17 Legal Ways to Double Your Income

Actionable tips from local, national, and international experts that can help you double your income.

Authors

Randy Bernstein

Christine Clifton

Leslie Flowers

Pete C. Goswick

Earl Hadden

Lisa Hall

Steve Hamm

Frank Manson

Brian K. McNeill

Diana M. Needham

Tim Pedersen

Marie Snider

Marie Snider (signature)

Copyright © 2014

17 Legal Ways to Double Your Income
Copyright © 2014 by Diana M. Needham, Earl Hadden, Marie Snider

www.17Legal WaysToDoubleYour Income.com

ISBN: 978-0-9894364-1-0

The publisher has strived to be as accurate and complete as possible in the creation of this book.

This book is not intended for use as a source of legal, business, accounting, or financial advice. All readers are advised to seek services of competent professionals in legal, business, accounting, and financial fields.

In practical advice books, as in anything else in life, there are no guarantees of income made. Readers are cautioned to rely on their own judgment about their individual circumstances and to act accordingly.

While all attempts have been made to verify information provided for this publication, the publisher assumes no responsibility for errors, omissions, or contrary interpretation of the subject matter herein. Any perceived slights of specific persons, peoples, or organizations are unintended.

Special Bonus From Diana, Earl, And Marie

Now that you have your copy of *17 Legal Ways to Double Your Income*, you are on your way to growing your business fast! Just pick one of the ways that resonates with you and take action to implement. Don't allow yourself to become overwhelmed by all 17! Just pick one and get moving.

You'll also receive the special bonus we created to provide another big dose of business inspiration ... Diana's *30-minute interview with Larry Winget*, filled with wisdom and insights about marketing your business and Larry's 3 Rules of Business. You'll receive access to not only the audio but the written transcript.

Not sure who Larry Winget is? He is a six-time *New York Times/Wall Street Journal* bestselling author and a member of the International Speaker Hall Of Fame. He has starred in his own television series and appeared in national television commercials. Larry is also a regular contributor on many news shows on the topics of money, personal success, parenting and business. Larry is also the trademarked **Pitbull of Personal Development®**.

While this interview is offered for sale, as a special bonus you can claim it for free here:

http://17LegalWaysToDoubleYourIncome.com/bookbonus/

We are in your corner. Let us know how we can help you further. Here's to doubling your income...fast!

Best,

Diana, Earl, and Marie

PREFACE

"Most people don't need to be taught, they just need to be reminded!" – Unknown

This project started with a group of coaches and mentors having coffee in the lobby of the Siena Hotel in Chapel Hill, NC. The topic had turned to why a few of our clients were remarkably successful, but most were just scraping by. The discussion was very animated as idea after idea that had worked for our clients were put on the table. Great ideas!

We realized that these ideas had been presented to all of our clients, but only a few of them have experienced dramatic results. As we talked about our most successful clients, we noticed some common characteristics:

They were willing to believe that they could achieve significant results – doubling or tripling their business or more.

They were willing to work to expand their "comfort zone" – to learn to do things in new and different ways.

They were willing to experiment.

They had a positive, "can do" attitude.

They were willing, in fact desired, to be held accountable.

One client discovered that he spent a tremendous amount of his "prime time" (the time when prospects were available) doing things that could easily be done in off hours – or better yet delegated or not done at all. By implementing the concept of IPAs (Income Producing Activities), he has doubled his income in just over a year.

Another owner of a small business, who had incurred a large debt and was working long hours (often more than 70 hours a week), had a similar experience. Analysis showed that his pricing was lower than his competition by about 25%, despite the fact that his reputation was the best in the market he served. By making his prices more competitive, his income has grown by over 50%, and he has more time to spend with his family (though he still puts in more time than most business owners, because he has a Big Hairy Audacious Goal!).

In this book, we take some of the concepts you have heard about many times (including some you have likely tried) plus a few new ones and give you a framework to implement them successfully. We are grateful for all of the local, national, and international experts who graciously contributed their wisdom to this book

Some readers will find a key that allows them to double their income in a very short period of time. Others will have to implement two or three of these methods over several months to get dramatic results. Unfortunately, some people will continue to dabble. They will try one thing, quit, and try something else or put up personal roadblocks. They won't see any improvement at all.

Let's be clear about this book

This book is for small business owners who serious about growing their businesses, serving their communities, and doubling their income...not someday but now. It is for business owners who want to experience amazing income and profit results, well beyond those they currently have in mind.

This book is not for entrepreneurs looking for a quick fix or the "make money overnight" ideas. There are plenty of sites and marketers online who will gladly sell you a product or program that makes this claim. Let the buyer beware! If it sounds too good to be true, it is.

Nor is this book for the business owner who is a hoarder of information and never takes action to implement. To those who have decided to wait until they have more training or finish the most recent marketing program they bought or book they are reading and have no sense of urgency to grow their business, don't let this book become part of your accumulated resources. Expecting a miracle to occur without taking any action is a delusion.

If you are committed to improving your business, this book is for you. If you are just dabbling, put it back on the shelf and move on.

One last thing:

The legal ways to double your income outlined in this book will enable you to move forward quickly.

Not all of them will apply or fit your business at this point in time. Identify just a few that are a good fit for your current goals and take action. Leave the rest for the next time you read this book and are looking for great ideas to implement.

In some chapters, there are blank spaces for you to fill in. Get a pen or pencil to fill in these blanks. Then get a highlighter to mark the sections that you want to come back to and remember. Use this book as a guide.

The book is organized into 4 categories: Planning and Organization, Sales, Marketing, and Online Marketing and Social Media. You may want to choose the topic area of most interest where you know you need more focus and start there.

This information is extremely valuable if you apply what you learn. You must take action. Make a commitment right now to take small continuous steps to double your business.

Let's get started.

CONTENTS

PREFACE 3

PLANNING AND ORGANIZATION

CHAPTER ONE *Improve your business every day* 11

CHAPTER TWO *Choose business associates carefully* 19

CHAPTER THREE *Accelerate your business growth* 27

CHAPTER FOUR *Focus on income producing activities* 41

CHAPTER FIVE *Implement the right systems & processes* 47

SALES

CHAPTER SIX *Differentiate yourself from your competition* ... 63

CHAPTER SEVEN *Sell big orders to big clients* 73

CHAPTER EIGHT *Ask for referrals* 81

MARKETING

CHAPTER NINE *Keep your marketing simple* 93

CHAPTER TEN *Create a sustainable lead generation system* . 107

CHAPTER ELEVEN *Make the perfect business impression* 119

CHAPTER TWELVE *Become a sought after speaker* 131

CHAPTER THIRTEEN *Cash in on credibility & authority* 139

CHAPTER FOURTEEN *Create momentum with promo products* 151

ONLINE MARKETING AND SOCIAL MEDIA

CHAPTER FIFTEEN *Leverage the power of video* 159

CHAPTER SIXTEEN *Build your 5-star reputation* 169

CHAPTER SEVENTEEN *Market your business online* 175

CONCLUSION 189

Planning and Organization

CHAPTER ONE

Commit to improving yourself and your business every day.
Earl Hadden

Continuous improvement is one of the most effective ways to double your income. If you're not moving ahead, you're falling behind.

When I first went to work at IBM, just after graduating from UNC, I encountered a slogan that has stuck with me over the years. "Work Smarter, Not Harder." It resonated with me because I preferred to use my brain to come up with easier solutions to problems than struggle to do things following a laborious, dull routine. (I must admit that occasionally my creativity caused more problems than it solved – but that's another story!)

A few years later, I asked Tony Lamia, a co-worker who ran the programming group for the software company where we worked, what he looked for in a new recruit. "I hire people who are smart and lazy," he said. "They figure out how to get the job done quickly without a lot of complexity."

Over the years, I found that clients put far more value on solutions to business opportunities than they did to a computer program or database system that just automated the existing system (what James Champy and Michael Hammer, in their book, *Reengineering The Corporation*, called "paving the cow path").

I worked with a team of people to develop a methodology (a repeatable process that will deliver consistent results). This methodology has been adopted by hundreds of companies and, according to one consulting company, has generated over $4 Billion in value for the companies who have used it.

This approach used concepts from dozens of industry thought leaders (meaning we borrowed from everybody!). It proved effective in just about every industry. But it was too large and complex for small businesses to use it.

When I retired from corporate consulting and started working with small businesses and independent professionals, I realized that they had similar problems and needed a consistent way to address them. So I developed a continuous improvement methodology just for them – taking out as much of the complexity as I could and streamlining the process so that it could be done by a solopreneur in the amount of time available. (My experience shows that most small business owners and independent professionals work 50 to 60 hours and can only make about 10% of that time available to work on improving their business. (You've probably heard the expression "working in the business, not on the business!"). That means that their improvement efforts can only take 5 or 6 hours a week! My goal was to help them work smarter, not harder.

So here's how the process works:

1. **Document your strategic goal**. This may be called a BHAG (Big Hairy Audacious Goal – Jim Collins' *Good to Great*), or Definite Major Purpose (from Napoleon Hill's *Think and Grow Rich!)*. It is the primary focus for a long (3 to 5 year) period of time. This goal must be specific! You must be able to see yourself attaining it in your "mind's eye". What rewards will you get when you achieve it? The popular terminology is your WHY, but this is often too unspecific to drive you to its realization.

2. **Define the one or two strategies you will follow to attain this** goal. What problem are you going to solve? Who (be very specific about this) are you going to provide this solution to? How will you solve this problem (product, service or a combination)? Are you going to provide the product or service or are you going to sell someone else's

products? Are there geographic targets or boundaries to the market you will serve? What is your high-level marketing approach to achieving these goals ("permission marketing", "pull vs. push")? What information will you need to successfully implement your plan? What is the income and expense model for this plan?

3. **Develop a "process model" for each strategy** (in some cases an activity might appear in the model for more than one strategy). The process model usually starts with 6 or 7 high level activities – plan the strategy, acquire resources, define and build the product/service, market the product (building a target market/product matrix), sell the product, deliver and provide service for the product, provide administrative services. Break each of the high level activities into smaller activities (each process "decomposes" into 5 – 7 activities, so now you have 25 – 49 activities).

4. **Identify 4 or 5 activities that are most important to achieve your BHAG (high level goal) and where you have a performance problem**. At this point, don't start trying to solve problems – you'll end up running around in circles.

5. **Determine whether any of these activities put the business at risk**. For example, under administrative services an activity might be remit sales taxes. Failure to do this will likely trigger the state or federal authorities to close your business.

6. **Identify the root cause of this performance problem**. (They may be pricing, overhead too high, cash mismanagement or any number of things). Select the improvement area.

7. **Develop a project plan for the improvement effort**. Define who needs to be involved, what tasks will be done and what measures will show that you are successful.

   History tells us that Ben Franklin started each year identifying 12 areas of his life that he wanted to improve. He would then prioritize them and list them by month with the most important put on his calendar for January and so on. At the end of each month, he would evaluate his progress and decide whether to move on to the next item or continue to work on the current issue for another month. Occasionally, he would come back to a topic previously worked on. (It is amazing how our unconscious mind continues to work on problems for us even when we are not aware that it is happening!).

   You may determine that your top item needs 60 days (or even 90 days – but no more!).

8. **Measure your progress and, on a monthly basis, determine whether your plan is working or that you need to change the plan to achieve the level of improvement you need.**

What is your most pressing problem? For many it is not enough quality referrals. For others it is pricing – too low and you work hard, but lose money on every sale. For others it is overhead – they are spending more that they can afford based on the level of sales that they have (though this might be the opposite side of the "not enough sales" problem. Only when you determine which problem area you are going to work on can you start to achieve significant business improvement.

Summary

My experience is that small business owners and independent professionals spend up to 80% of their time working on the wrong things. Once you identify the High Performance Activities and Income Producing Activities, you can apply your effort to fewer activities and "Work Smarter, Not Harder..

So my tip for helping you double your income is:

Commit to improving yourself and your business every day. Continuous improvement is one of the most effective ways to double your income.

Ideas for Action:

Work with a mentor or coach to identify your personal and business improvement areas and put together an improvement plan for each area. Pick the one that will have the most impact and focus all of your available management time (your "working on the business" time) on that project.

Enlist an accountability partner to help you stay on track. It is easy to start chasing squirrels, especially if the improvement project is not in one of your favorite parts of the business.

Find someone who specializes in the area you must improve and ask them for help.

Measure your progress along the way. Have goals that are daily, weekly and monthly. Have a visual scorecard that you see frequently to help keep you focused.

Earl Hadden

Like many entrepreneurs, Earl Hadden's career as an entrepreneur and coach started when he got fired. Earl had worked in the Information Technology field for 11 years working up from an entry level programmer at IBM, through the sales and sales management ranks to Vice President of R&D for one of the top software companies. He had recently been recruited by a small software company to be the VP of Sales when the owner decided to eliminate the entire management team that he had just hired.

The timing couldn't have been better. Several of Earl's former clients had approached him about helping them with projects, and Earl's small business owner career started in the spare bedroom. It grew to 30+ consultants and work in over 24 countries.

Earl's team worked on methods and techniques for database design for large systems and evolved to analytics and information quality. During that time, Earl read Reengineering the Corporation, one of the top management books of the last 50 years. A key message that got his attention was "Don't automate any process until it has been reengineered." It went on to talk about companies that "Paved the Cow Path". So Earl's company added Process Improvement to its methods. This soon overtook technology as the major offering of the company.

In 2003, Earl retired from corporate consulting and with his wife, Fran, moved back to his home state of North Carolina. After several years of unsuccessful attempts to improve his golf game, Earl started the Small Business Success Project. He applies lessons learned from starting and operating three small businesses (from "solopreneurs" to nearly $4 million in sales) and methods from his corporate consulting experience to companies ranging from startups to $5 million in sales.

A recent client survey identified these key benefits people had gained working with Earl:

Focus – identifying 4 – 5 key activities (IPAs or Income Producing Activities) and making them the top priorities every day.

Pricing – how to value products and services, convey that value to a "tribe" and generate more income from every client.

Process – improving the way key processes are performed, making them more profitable while delegating low value activities to others.

Earl is an avid student of religion and anything to do with business or personal improvement. He and Fran have two married daughters and an 8 year old grandson and live in a small town outside Chapel Hill. He is still working on his golf game.

You can connect with Earl Hadden on

LinkedIn (www.linkedin.com/in/earlhadden) or at

www.17LegalWaysToDoubleYourIncome.com

CHAPTER TWO

Choose your colleagues and business associates carefully.
Earl Hadden

In five years your income will be the average of the five people you spend the most time with. Choose your colleagues and business associates carefully. Make sure that they have the same values as yours.

Integrity, Reliability, Desire to Serve Others, and Commitment to Growth are all important qualities for the people on my team.

Some people lift me up, others drag me down. Some waste my time, others inspire me to do more than I've ever been able to get done. Some challenge my paradigm – that collection of opinions, experiences and beliefs that provide the framework for who I look at what I do and how I do it.

Have you ever taken time to think about the people around you and how they impact your effectiveness? This chapter looks at selecting the best people to be part of your team -- some as mentors and coaches, some as associates or colleagues and others as your support team.

I first started thinking about the question of the people around me when one of my early mentors told me "In five years, your income will be the average of the five people you spend the most time with." The more I thought about that wise advice, the more I realized that I had to find some new people to hang out with! Part of that realization was that I needed to spend more time where successful people were.

I had just moved into sales from the programming department of a mid-size software company. My usual lunch group was other programmers and support staff – fun people, but not living the lifestyle I wanted to live. While I kept my old pals, I started having lunch two or three days a week with the sales team which included managers who were very successful.

Outside work, I also needed to make some changes. I joined a duplicate bridge group (I played a lot – maybe too much – in school!) and a tennis group. The people in these groups were much more successful than the folks on my darts team. (HFTB – Here for the beer.)

One thing I failed to realize at the time (after all, I was only about 24 years young!) was what values did I want the people around me to have. Back then, I was looking mostly at financial success. Of course, when you are just out of school and don't have any money – and are driving a dark blue car without air conditioning in Los Angeles – that's usually the first thing that acts as a motivator.

Looking back, I now know that I should have started by defining the values that are important to me, and then looked for people that met that profile. Early in my career my values were my Mercedes, expensive vacations, and lots of nice clothes. Over time, my values have shifted as I have learned more about myself and the world around me.

My work with small business owners and independent professionals had shown that very few people think about this question. They are "stuck" in their family situation, their business is flat or declining, they are frustrated and often down on themselves because the success they desire continues to elude them.

As one of the people I was coaching at one point said "It feels like I'm in a hole and I just can't stop digging!" When I start working with someone on improving their business results, I find that they are working hard – some of them 50, 60 or 70 hours a week...but they're not making any progress toward their view of success.

I realized that one of the keys to success, one of the ways a person can double his or her income, is to build a team that supports the achievement of a Big Hairy Audacious Goal.   To me, the characteristics I value most are:

Integrity

Reliability/Consistency

Desire to Serve Others

Commitment to Growth

To me, Integrity incorporates several characteristics. As the train children's book, it means "I say what I do and I do what I say." A person has integrity if he can be counted on. One of the reasons this is so important to me is that this is an area where I struggle. I see myself as a "big picture guy" – loads of great ideas, but I run out of interest or energy (or both) before reaching the finish line. One of the reasons that this characteristic is at the top of my list is that people with great integrity help me demonstrate this characteristic myself.

The second characteristic is Reliability or Consistency. This means that their message, and their answers to my questions are based on strong beliefs. From these people I don't hear "it depends" very often. They know what they should do – and can help me stay clear in my message.

Desire to Serve Others is a little different, but equally important. The people in my inner circle are more committed to helping others be successful. They know that, to quote Zig Ziglar, "if they help enough other people get what they want, they will get what they want." One aspect of this characteristic is that people with a Desire to Serve Others spend most of their time talking about others' success and less time talking about what is important to themselves.

Commitment to Growth is really about applying continuous improvement techniques to their own life. We have a choice whether we are satisfied to be "as is" or "new and improved" every day. I value those who learn, who stretch the boundaries of their comfort zone and who teach those around them every day.

Here's our approach that will link your values with your results and help you double your income. Define your values and rank how you are doing towards those values.

What values are most important to you? Identify 5 – 7 values that are really important to you. The Boy Scout Law is a good place to start. A Scout is:

Trustworthy	Obedient
Loyal	Cheerful
Helpful	Thrifty
Friendly	Brave
Courteous	Clean
Kind	Reverent

Some other characteristics on my list are

Team player	Enthusiastic
Service to others – puts others first	Creative
	Moderate
Completes projects on time	Energetic

What other values/characteristics are important to you?

_____

_____

_____

_____

Once you have identified your 5 – 7 values, rank the importance of each one (using a 10 point scale where 10 is most important, 9 is next most importance, and so on. You may not use a number more than once.) Next, rank how satisfied you are with your performance on the ones on your list (using the same 10 point scale).

Values / Characteristics	Importance (10=most)	Performance (10=best)

Once you have established your values and done a "self-assessment", look at the people that make up your circle of mentors, associates and supporters. Do the complement your strengths? Do they raise you up, or do they bring you down?

What additional roles do you need to fill on your team? Many small business owners try to do everything on their own. This is a failing approach. You need to focus your time on the things that you do extremely well and that only you can do. Other activities should be outsourced (sometimes even delegating them upward!). Ensure that everyone in your circle shares your values. They will help you improve your performance and will hold you accountable.

Let me share an example of where assuming someone on a team was committed to our shared values cost the whole team support from management. A few years ago, I worked on a project for a pharmaceutical company. Our team had a tight deadline. The benefits of bringing the project in on time were essential to the success of our client. Several of the people on the team had been assigned to the team and, as we found out later, didn't agree with the project objective. We had problems getting them to show up for meetings. And after missing a meeting, they would take up much of the next meeting re-hashing the items agreed upon in the meeting they missed. The schedule slipped as we had to re-do documents. We missed the due date and overran the budget. The people who were not committed to the success of the project were not held responsible, and the people who worked the hardest were blamed for the failure.

We learned that we must define the project objectives, the value of success (and the cost of failure), and gain commitment from each participant before starting. If someone cannot commit to the project objectives, we cannot afford to have them on the team.

Summary

Before you start any major project, revisit the list of characteristics that you value. Apply those characteristics to each member of the team, and make sure that everyone fits. In his book, Good to Great, Jim Collins says that one of the most important keys to success is to "get the right people on the bus, the wrong people off the bus, and the right people in the right seats." We also need to make sure that everyone on the bus wants to take the trip.

So my tip for helping you double your income is:

Choose your business associates carefully – make sure that they have similar values to yours. Integrity, Reliability, Desire to Serve Others, Commitment to Growth are all important qualities for the people on my team.

Ideas for Action:

Go back to the list of the characteristics you value. Next to each one, write the name of two or three of your associates who are excellent in that category.

Now think about a recent project that didn't go so well. Were there any people on the team that didn't demonstrate those characteristics? If you have anyone on this list, you should discuss your concerns with them. If they understand the problem, and agree to improve in that area, you will have started moving toward a long term relationship. If they don't agree, it's time to look for a new team member.

Finally, take a few minutes to look again at your performance on the characteristics. Develop a personal action plan to improve in those areas where your performance falls short.

See Chapter 1 for Earl Hadden's biography.

CHAPTER THREE

Surround yourself with like minded people to create consistent, predictable, and accelerated business growth.
Leslie Flowers

Follow the age-old steps to create a mastermind that provides the specialized knowledge you do not already possess to get your business moving forward quickly.

The Power of Mastermind

Did you know that Andrew Carnegie (1835-1919) considered the greatest industrialist in the United States attributed his entire fortune to the power accumulated through his mastermind?[1]

Entering the steel business in the 1870's, "In 1901, he sold the Carnegie Steel Company to banker John Pierpont Morgan for $480 million."[2]

The personal proceeds he received for the sale of his company was equivalent to about 1 per cent of US GDP at the time. In proportionate terms that would make Carnegie richer than America's two wealthiest men, Warren Buffett and Bill Gates, combined today.[3]

---

[1] Hill, Napoleon (1936). Chapter 10, Power of the Master Mind, The Driving Force in J. Ross Cornwell (Ed.) Think and Grow Rich! The Original Version, Restored and Revised. 2007 (177). Chula Vista, CA: Aventine Press.

[2] http://www.history.com/topics/andrew-carnegie

[3] Thornhill, John (2014) The story of Skibo, Andrew Carnegie's Scottish estate. www.ft.com

According to Napoleon Hill, author of Think and Grow Rich, the best selling self-help book of all time, mastermind is defined as the "Coordination of knowledge and effort, in a spirit of harmony, between two or more people, for the attainment of a definite purpose."[4]

I learned about Think and Grow Rich in 2008 and have been facilitating in-depth mastermind studies on Hill's work since that time.

In early 2008, already an avid student and teacher of personal transformation and development for ten years, I landed on the work of Napoleon Hill and Think and Grow Rich and began to facilitate face to face weekly mastermind studies of the work.

After facilitating my first dozen multi week masterminds in the first 18 months, I began to notice my own thinking had changed. And I also began to Believe in the principles I was teaching ... from my own results and those of mastermind participants. One thing of which I am absolute sure: Our results are always the exact reflection of what we believe.

The more I saw proof that these timeless principles work, the more Faith I had in them and the more I could leverage them to influence my own results.

There is no doubt that over the 200 or so generations since recording history, the mastermind concept shows up wherever there is success.

Alexander the Great (Greece 356-323BC) had a group of advisors that by today's terms would be considered a mastermind.

Napoleon Hill, in his classic Think and Grow Rich, focused on the 'power of mastermind' and refers to it as one of the thirteen key principles of success. Written almost 100 years ago, Andrew

[4] Ibid., 176.

Carnegie commissioned Hill (sans salary), a then 20-year-old reporter, to repeatedly interview some 500 our country's greatest successes to find out what they were doing to achieve success ... that everyone else who was not successful failed to do.

Think and Grow Rich is the synthesis of timeless business principles when applied in business can handily produce a millionaire. Published in 1937, the 1960 edited version has sold over 100 million copies, making it the most read self-help book of all time.[5]

As you are reading this chapter, it may occur to you to wonder why — if Think and Grow Rich touts the full blueprint for success — aren't there as many millionaires as copies sold?

The answer? Even with the simply stated steps in the classic and with documented, palpable and amazing results over the last 100 years, people still "do not do what they know to do."

I would be remiss in excluding Benjamin Franklin in the history of mastermind. In 1727 Franklin created a discussion "Junto" (Spanish for council) based on his 13 Virtues of Living, two centuries before Hill wrote Think and Grow Rich. Franklin's Mastermind lasted 40 years!

Andrew Carnegie "... attributed his entire fortune to the POWER he accumulated through this 'Master Mind'."[6]

A mastermind alliance speeds up success. You don't have to learn to do everything because likely there is a mastermind participant that has that skill, or knows someone who does. You get to focus on your endpoint, your goal, and not interrupt your flow of work in that direction. This is a new way of thinking.

---

[5] The Napoleon Hill Foundation. http://www.naphill.org/
[6] Ibid., 177.

More and more of us are working alone, and we are used to doing everything ourselves. We jump from tasks to grow our businesses (getting clients and other income producing activities) to tasks that keep our businesses running (managing administrative tasks such as bookkeeping, web site updates, etc.). Time is traded and lost ... time that we never get back. We cannot predict our monthly income and the idea of gaining momentum and consistent growth is not even on our radar. It leaves us frustrated and often disillusioned. No one to talk to. No one to trust. No one to share ideas and get feedback. No safe place.

Even when I share with you in this chapter HOW to construct and operate your own business mastermind, you likely will do nothing. The performance gap is a phenomenon — knowing what to do and still not doing it. And we even add more and more information to the mix (books, workshops, seminars) ... with which we do little if anything as well.

The paradox is that being in a fully functioning business mastermind has you break through your performance gap ... so you actually begin 'doing' what you already know to do, and you put to work new information that comes your way to move you to your desired endpoint ... your goal. Amazing.

7 Key BENEFITS of Mastermind
1. Collaborative tasks and talents. By sharing talents with mastermind participants you get to focus on your expertise.
2. Reduce learning curve. Because others are supporting you with their expertise and wisdom, you don't have to trade your time to learn 'everything.'
3. Gain experience, skill, and confidence. Practice gives us experience and skill. Continued successes and business

traction builds our confidence in our ability to be a successful business owner.

4. See real visible progress in business. When you are focused on your business goal and not distracted by tasks that 'need doing' that are not your expertise, you can calculate business growth.

5. Instant, valuable support network. You are not sure which company provides the best service. You can pick up the phone or send an email to your mastermind partners and get a trusted instant answer.

6. Consistent accountability system. The best results come from touching base with a 'partner' several times each week. Both people have the goals of the other to assure tasks are being met on time.

7. Develop values of integrity, honesty, and compassion. When you are trusted over time and you do what you say you will do by when you say you will do it, you are developing character and real authenticity.

A business mastermind sounds like a pretty good idea, right? If you are beginning to think about the benefits of starting your own mastermind, what do you need to know? Who is the right 'partner' for your mastermind? How can you tell?

Make your 1st Step to identify people that have the attributes listed below.

Step 1: Who is the right mastermind partner?

7 Attributes of the Ideal Mastermind Participant

1. Share a common interest with each participant. If you are in real estate, having a participant who is a university professor may not be the best choice for someone to listen to you and give you feedback on your ideas.
2. Is committed to the success of all participants. Each person must want to and strive to maintain positive outcomes, not only for themselves, but for each participant.
3. Has similar skill and/or success level. If you are a c-level exec, having the mail room clerk on your mastermind may not be a good match.
4. Welcomes accountability. Few of us are really great at doing what we know to do 'when no one is looking.' Being held to task consistently and repeatedly over time by your mastermind partners helps develop the discipline required to achieve success.
5. Wants to exceed their goals. A mastermind participant thinks very big, never reduces their goal based on outside conditions and circumstance, and in fact often expands the goal.
6. Trusts group feedback. You want your participants to be someone you trust to give you honest feedback.
7. Takes action on ideas and innovations from the group. During a mastermind dialogue very often other members will come up with ideas for your goal! This is true master-minding. It's allowing others to contribute to your project and being good with that.

Now you are beginning to understand how the benefits of working in unison with like minded people actually accelerates your performance!

Now it's time to lay the foundation for your mastermind ... your operating procedures, Step 2. You are there to get to the point quickly and effectively. You are there to listen for what the person speaking is 'not seeing.' We cannot see ourselves from inside the picture frame ... but trusted mastermind partners can do this handily.

By leaving the gate together (all moving toward your business goal) and having a specific plan for your mastermind, you will waste no valuable time and enjoy the benefits of an accelerating business.

You have the benefits of mastermind, how to select participants for maximum effectiveness, and if you wish to go further, lay a solid operating foundation.

Step 2: What are the Foundational Principles of your mastermind?

3 KEYS for Successful Mastermind Participation

1. Develop a mission, vision, and/or purpose statement. If the group does not know where it's going, what the participants want, you have no focus, and you will be wasting time in confusion.

2. Set an endpoint goal (large) with monthly milestones. You can set this for yourself and for the group itself.
[In 1979, interviewers asked new graduates from the Harvard's MBA Program and found that: 84% had no specific goals at all, 13% had goals but they were not committed to paper, 3% had clear, written goals and plans to accomplish them. In 1989, the interviewers again interviewed the graduates of that class. You can guess the results: The

13% of the class who had goals were earning, on average, twice as much as the 84 percent who had no goals at all, and even more staggering – the three percent who had clear, written goals were earning, on average, ten times as much as the other 97 percent put together.][7]

3. Earmark time each week for the Mastermind. Schedule mastermind meeting time at the same time each week. Treat the appointment like your most valuable client. Only allow an emergency that only you can handle to keep you from that meeting.

If you 1) decide to develop your own mastermind, 2) you know how to identify the 'right' participants, and 3) you have set the operating foundation for effectiveness, the last thing you need to get started is for everyone to agree to ways of operating inside the mastermind.

Step 3: What are your mutual agreements?

7 Agreements for Mastermind Participant Excellence

1. Develop an "Oath of Intention" to be read before each meeting. Typically it is your mission or vision ... the outcome of working together in a business mastermind.

2. Determine day of week, time, and how long sessions will last. Set a repeating appointment.

3. Keep sessions between 60 and 90 minutes; start and end on time. Less than 60 minutes is not enough and by the time you

---

[7] McCormack, Mark H. (1986). What They Don't Teach You at Harvard Business School: Notes From a Street-Smart Executive.1984. New York, NY: Bantam Books

hit 90 minutes, you are on sensory overload. No need to go further at that time.

4. Communicate if unable to attend. Allow no interruptions.

5. Maintain a collaborative, rather than competitive state of mind. Two CPAs in the same mastermind? Why not? Both CPAs have their own unique style and will resonate with some and not others. Mastermind partners refer one another. Competition? None exists. If you began serving all the people who truly need your services, 24/7/365 within a 50 mile radius, you could NEVER serve them all.

6. Leave the Mastermind if these agreements can no longer be met. If you find you are out of integrity and you are not meeting the agreements, simply say so. If it doesn't feel right for you, you can be sure your partners feel something similar. Step away.

7. Be your Word: do what you say you will do by when you say you will do it. Give a later finish date and come in early with more than expected. Be honest and responsible. The mastermind is a proving and training ground for building character in all areas of your life.

So is this possible for you? Of course it is ... if you want it and are willing. I know there is a lot of how-to information here. Simply start with Step #1 and go point by point. Make it easy. You don't have to 'leap' out of the gate ... you may walk ... just keep moving your feet.

I do want to share a Case Study (2009 - Present) of one mastermind's impact on society so you get the idea of what is possible for you and your business associates. These people simply did what I instructed them to do. They took that one step first and the rest is history in the making.

2009. Mastermind convened end of summer. Directions were: Stay together. They followed directions.

1. The next year, this mastermind created People-Builders, Inc, a 501 (c) (3) non-profit assisting 5 families in getting back on their financial feet. They ...

    1-1 built 2 homes for returning veterans with missing limbs or severely disabled

    2-1 provided school supplies for children in need

    3-1 fed the homeless on countless occasions

    4-1 supported and hit the Guinness World Record for "most food collected in one single event"

    5-1 received the Presidential Citation award for community service.

2. They developed life-long friendships and support group.

3. They are launching a new tech start-up with the goal for being the next SAP or Amazon.

4. Together they have shared life changes in marriage and family and are now teaching their children the power of love and giving to others.

Napoleon Hill, the man who really brought the world 'mastermind' into our everyday vocabulary, states in Think and Grow Rich, "No two minds ever come together without, thereby, creating a third, invisible, intangible force which may be likened to a third mind."[8]

Starting a business mastermind based on participant criteria above — sharing common interest, being committed to everyone's

---

[8] Ibid., 176.

success, possessing similar success or skill levels, welcoming accountability, exceeding goals and trusting group feedback — gives you a sound and solid foundation yielding an "express to business success!"

With everyone in agreement to honor the agreements of the mastermind, you will be following the same path or blueprint for success as all the great successes throughout history. You will be doing what most people do not do. And you will be enjoying the benefits of a mastermind that is personally fulfilling and financially rewarding.

- Where are you now on the subject?
- Are you thinking of starting your own mastermind?
- Do you have enough information to start one?
- Should you join one already in operation?
- Who do you know that you trust that you would like to mastermind with?

Before you take any action, sit and think about those questions and jot down with pen your thoughts at the end of this chapter. I say with pen and not keyboard ... here's why:

When you write on paper, you slow down and begin to think. As you are thinking most people see pictures about what they are writing. Lovely images make us feel great and not so pretty ones make us feel down (keep them lovely). When we begin to take action the results we get always are a 100% match to what you are feeling (feeling is believing).

1. **Where are you now on the subject?**

2. **Are you thinking of starting your own mastermind?**

3. **Do you have enough information to start one?**

4. **Should you join one already in operation?**

5. **Who do you know that you trust that you would like to mastermind with?**

Leslie Flowers

Leslie Flowers is an author, presenter and advisor who empowers people to tap their genuine inspiration, plan for success and achieve their fullest potential. She works with entrepreneurs, team leaders and executives to identify values build high-performance teams, reach consensus on strategy and more.

As a young woman, Leslie lived in San Francisco and served as a flight attendant during the Vietnam War. At 30,000 feet, she hosted troops flying from the United States into war zones and back.

She spent 45 years working for businesses from lean start-up to corporate enterprise. There, she grew her skills in writing, production and publishing. Her attention to detail and quality earned her executive respect as a trustworthy brand steward. Her direction of a proposal and production team for one small business won a $30 million contract that put the company on the map.

Leslie developed her core leadership strengths during 20 years of immersion in multiple transformational techniques for personal growth and positive change. A key influence on her work was Napoleon Hill, author of the timeless best-selling book on personal success, *Think and Grow Rich!*, originally released in 1937.

"Leslie and I have discussed Napoleon Hill's life and work extensively. This lady knows what she is talking about."

-J. Ross Cornwell, editor of Think and Grow Rich! The Original Version Restored and Revised and first editor-in-chief of Think & Grow Rich Newsletter, a Napoleon Hill Foundation publication.

Leslie started her own business to show others how to come "face to face with their infinite potential." Since 2008, she has facilitated more than 35 in-person "mastermind" studies on the principles of success and goal achievement for hundreds. Each 10-week study trains participants to tap their interests, pursue their passions and achieve their personal goals. Participants have used her training to start their own businesses, write and sell best-selling books and more.

"The most important take-away from my work with mastermind participants is that even when we know what it takes to succeed and we understand it, we rarely take the steps necessary to achieve it," says Leslie. "We start by identifying barriers to success so we can transform them, accelerate achievement and consistently achieve high performance."

Leslie is mother of two children and grandmother of four. She loves to entertain guests in her dream home on a lake, a vision she held for five years and brought into reality through her work. She enjoys spending time with her grandchildren and has a passion for empowering others to develop success skills and achieve their greatest potential.

For more information, visit Leslie Flowers on LinkedIn or on her website, www.leslie-flowers.com.

CHAPTER FOUR

Identify the income producing activities that you must perform (and perform well) and focus your efforts on them for success.
Earl Hadden

Research and experience prove that business owners and independent professionals spend as much as 80% of their time working on the wrong things – define your Income Producing Activities and focus your efforts on them.

In my years of corporate consulting, I spent a lot of time studying processes and process improvement. Large organizations have some interesting challenges, including:

- Defining (and gaining consensus on) their processes (There can be over 1,000 activities in a single organization!)
- Identifying who does what on each process (who Authorizes it, who is Responsible for performing it; who will provide Expertise; who are the Workers; and who needs to be Informed of progress – AREWI);
- What information is required to perform each process (and who can Create, Read, Update and Delete it);
- Reaching agreement on which processes should be improved and who should be involved in fixing them;
- Agreeing on measurements to be used to determine success.

As you can imagine, a lot of politics and personal interests (for example, who is going to get a raise or promotion) come into play.

The issues for individual business owners and professionals are not as complex, but they can still take a lot of time and cause a lot of chaos! A typical small business will have 50 to 100 processes that it must successfully execute. Without an understanding of these process requirements, and a plan to get them performed, things will fall through the cracks. Some of these activities that fall through the cracks will cost you money; others will alienate customers or partners; still others will cause regulatory or legal issues with a whole range of unpleasant ramifications.

Here's the approach our team developed to understand and improve processes for small businesses and independent professionals.

1. Define your Big Hairy Audacious Goal (BHAG) or Primary Purpose or Strategic Goal. This should be a 3 to 5 year goal. It is the primary WHY that you are in business. You should only have one or two Strategic Goals, more than that will lead to dilution of effort and ultimate failure.

2. Identify the high level activities (usually 5 – 7) that you must execute to achieve your BHAG. These represent HOW you plan to accomplish your Strategic Goal and usually include:
   • Plan the Business
   • Acquire Facilities and Resources
   • Design and Develop Products and/or Services
   • Market and Sell Products and/or Services
   • Deliver and Support Products and/or Services
   • Administer the Business

3. Identify the one or two Strategies that you are going to pursue to attain your BHAG. Strategies can include selecting specialty products, specific geographical markets, distribution channels, groups of customers (called "tribes") etc. If you have two Strategic Goals, the Strategies can overlap or may be unique for each goal. You will probably pursue a Strategy for multiple years. Organizations or

individuals who change Strategies too often have poor results.

4. Based on your Strategies, refine the high-level activities. For example, if you are going to pursue a specific "tribe", how are you going to market to them-? Each high-level activity usually "decomposes" into 3 to 7 activities. (Note: You now have 18 – 42 activities defined.)

5. Based on your Strategies (from step 3), develop your 1 year goals. These goals are more specific and may include number of sales, income amount, employees, etc.

6. Further decompose the activities that are needed to accomplish your 1 year goals. Use the 3 – 7 rule for decomposition, but only consider the activities that you are going to need.

At this point you will have 50 to 100 activities so you will need to rank them in terms of both importance to achieving your goals (1 year, Strategic and BHAG) and your current performance. There are two techniques to use here. The first is called the "positive/negative impact factor," and the second is called "Strength/Weakness/Opportunity/Threat" or SWOT analysis.

The "positive/negative impact factor" is the easier of the two. Each activity (all 50 to 100 of them) is assessed in terms of how it affects the success of the business – that is, how well it helps us achieve our goals. If poor performance on a particular activity could put us out of business, or put us in jail!) it gets a score of -5. On the other hand, if excellent performance on a particular activity would make us successful beyond our wildest dreams, it gets a score of +5. As you can imagine, there aren't many - -5 or +5. Most things fall toward the middle of the scale.

Positive/Negative Impact Factor

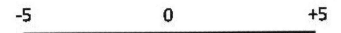

-5   0   +5

Items between -5 and 0 are called "hygiene factors". If you do a great job, nobody notices. But if you don't get it done, everybody notices (and complains loudly). A good example of a "hygiene factor" is payroll.

Items between 0 and +5 are "strategic initiatives. The higher the score, the better the results.

Do you have any -4s or -5s? If you do, drop everything else and get working on them. The closer you can get to 0 the better. Of course, getting a score above 0 doesn't help, so our goal is to spend the least amount of time and money to move these activities up the scale.

Do you have any +4s or +5s? Great! Pour it on! This is where you will have the most positive impact on your business.

SWOT Analysis is a more refined way to establish priorities. Again we list all of our activities. In the second column we rank them by importance to achieving our goal (using a 10 point scale where 10 is high and 1 is low). To ensure an equal spread of the results, divide the total number of activities on the list by 10 (if you have 50 activities, your number will be 5). You may use each number on the 10 point scale 5 times. The 5 most important activities get a score of 10 and so on down to the 5 least important being scored 1.

Next, add a column to rate your performance on each of the activities. Use the same process as we did for importance to develop a relative ranking.

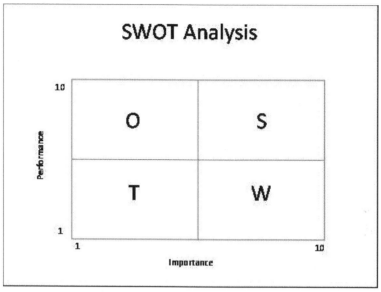

The last step in the SWOT Analysis is to plot each activity onto a grid (above). Those activities with high importance and high performance are Strengths. The ones with high importance are Weaknesses. Low importance, high performance activities are Opportunities, and low importance, low productivity are Threats.

First look at the Weaknesses. These are important, and we aren't doing very well. We need to work on these first. After we have improved all the Weaknesses, we can look at Strengths to determine whether they need to be improved. In theory, we would then look at Opportunities and then Threats; but in reality, we never get to those unless something changes in our business environment that causes our importance score to change.

Having completed these two analysis techniques, we can identify the activities that contribute the most to our success and make sure that we put these on our calendar before anything else.

Next steps

What is your BHAG or 5 year plan?

_____

_____

_____

What are the measures you will use to determine whether you are succeeding?

_____

_____

_____

What are the one or two Strategies that you will pursue?

_____

_____

_____

What are your 4 or 5 Income Producing Activities that you must do every day to ensure your overall success?

_____

_____

_____

See Chapter 1 for Earl Hadden's biography.

CHAPTER FIVE

**The right systems and processes are the keys to
successful, manageable growth.
Lisa Hall**

**Clearly identify the key steps to complete each big project.
Record each detailed step and create a procedure for use the
next time that function has to be completed. Delegation is easier
when there is a defined process to follow.**

When a big project gets presented to you, what do you do? This
is a real opportunity, and you know it could mean more business for
your company but you already have a few projects on your plate.
This new opportunity has a deadline that's just around the corner, but
in the back of your head a little voice says, "**never** turn down an
opportunity."

What do you do? Panic? Say NO? Take the opportunity, but
spend more time worrying about how to manage it with your busy
schedule than you actually spend working on the project itself?

The truth is when you are in charge of your own company you
really cannot let a good opportunity pass you by. If it's an
opportunity that is aligned with your values and will help you get
your business closer to your goals, then it's something you are going
to have to figure out a way to manage.

Here is what I know as a business coach. Many business owners
are overwhelmed or panicked if they even consider putting more
than one project on their plate at a time. That is not an effective way
to run a business. In fact running a business one project at a time will
quickly cause your business to fail. As a business owner, you must
become skilled at juggling more than one ball in the air at all times.

In fact, you may even find that -- like a circus -- you may have many different rings or departments you have to manage at the same time, and each of those have many people juggling several balls in the air at one time. The more talented you are at delegation and project planning, the better you will be at building your business and creating the income you desire and deserve.

No business survives with one service area or project line. But every day in my practice I hear things like, "when I finish my blog I will put out a newsletter." Or I hear, "once I've built my content for my program, I will get started writing my book." If you cannot have one area of focus at a time, I wonder if you have a business at all, or is it really just a hobby? Look to entrepreneurial companies that have had big success and you'll quickly see that even early on they were managing multiple projects and business functions at the same time.

So how do you go about making it all work without causing yourself loss of sleep and burnout? First of all, you have to remember that nothing happens overnight. You can't jump from juggling one project to handling 20 just like that, but what you can begin to do over time is to build some structure around processes and procedures for your business that will allow you to structure your time and allow you to delegate areas of your business and your projects to individuals who can finish them appropriately.

Before I became a small business coach, I worked for a company based out of California. This company managed a marketing product that a large and well-known business coach sold as one of his upsell products at events and to private coaching clients. The manager of this marketing division was a great guy, smart but not very tech savvy. When his part of the business was just beginning he could manage to keep records of commissions owned to the sales team members on paper, and he could have daily "check-ins" by phone to see where a project was and who on the creative team was currently working on it. But as the business began to take on more and more projects, this pen and phone method of project management became overwhelming; it was a matter of having no formal systems and no automation to keep systems running without much interaction by management. It kept the business stuck in a no growth mode for a long time.

With more growth opportunities projected and a desire to manage this growth effectively, I was brought in to create the operations department and get it organized so that the company could handle its processes efficiently to support a larger client base and make more money. So where do you even start to begin a process such as this? What I did and what I recommend to my clients is that you first begin by making a list of all of the tasks and procedures you have in your business that need to be done on a regular basis. For this operations department, commissions needed to be organized and paid on time, a system of project tracking needed to be developed so that we always knew who was working on a client's marketing project and at what stage it was in the process and a system was needed that would let us know what our daily expenses were and what our expected income was for each day was and a variety of other large processes. I had to watch, question, research and learn for some time. Then I started to make lists of the systems we needed to build.

Once I had my list of "tasks," I then set out to prioritize them. I needed to ask myself (and the company owner) a few questions around this process. These are questions I'd certainly recommend you ask yourself as well as you begin to think about delegation and system development.

What process if organized first would lead to an increase in income?

Which process when in place would lead to reduced time and effort?

Which process would lead to greater client satisfaction?

Which processes if put in place would allow delegation of some of the functions in the business?

Were there any processes that if done immediately would lead to a more positive customer experience?

After discovering the answers to these questions, we began by putting processes in place that would create more customer satisfaction because that was our number one area of weakness. If the clients were happy because we had put in place a system that let them check in with their creative team, see where their project was at all times, and allowed them to know when their payments were expected and the project would be completed, then they would be happier with the overall process. Our clients would then tell others about the company and give great testimonials. So that's where I began to unravel the unorganized processes that were in place and create streamlined systems to help manage virtually every process in that organization.

Organizing a business that had at this point about 1 million in sales a year and was about 7 years old, was a big undertaking, but it was manageable with patience and time. If your business is still a one or even a five-man show, it will be easier for you -- I promise! If your business is at the same point as the business above was when I began to work with them, you can still get your processes and procedures clearly identified and spelled out by working on one system at a time. But you should strongly consider hiring someone to work on this project specifically. It's not something I'd recommend you, as the CEO, work on because it will eat up your time and take you away from working in your area of brilliance, where your true money making activity is.

So let's break down the process and get you started on creating some processes for your own business. No matter what level you are at, the system for creating these processes are the same.

Create a list of tasks in your business that would be beneficial to delegate. Remember these tasks are those things in your business that you do not need to have your hands on or those tasks that do not fall in your area of expertise. What would be better to have someone else do because they could do it better than you and faster than you could? When working with my clients I advise them to keep a notepad with them at all times for about two weeks. Each time they perform a task for their business, they are instructed to write that task in their notebook. This will give you a clear picture of everything you do in your business. I guarantee if you do not do this step, you will miss some tasks. I know you probably do many tasks in your business, almost on autopilot, on a routine basis.

Prioritize these tasks by order of importance for delegation. What task if delegated to someone else would save you the most time and or result in an influx of revenue? Or what tasks on this list are burdensome for you and you know someone skilled in this particular area could do this task in a whole lot less time?

Take just one task from your prioritized list and create the steps in the process of completion.

The next time you or an employee performs this task, keep a document and clearly identify all of the steps in the process of that task. Keep the steps short and identify all information that will be needed to complete each step – e.g. passwords, websites, online apps, etc.

As a checkpoint, when this task is done again use the list process sheet you've created to perform the process as you've written it down. This is a time to put in additional steps and to catch any errors or parts of the process you may have skipped.

Next have someone else run through the task to be performed (alongside the person that's been completing the task) using the checklist you've created to see if they can exactly replicate the end product. A great thing to do here is to allow the person who would take over the process for a day or two if the employee in charge of the task were out sick.

Make any corrections and identify any trouble areas in directions to make sure everything is clearly spelled out. Step #5 should help you identify any trouble in language or any steps that are unclearly written.

Clean up your checklist, place it in your process and procedures folder and find the correct person to delegate this process to.

Remember, based on the size of the task or project you are delegating the above process could take a couple of days or need to be spread out over a few weeks' time. This is a process that you will need to have some patience to undertake, but once you begin to delegate the tasks, you will end up saving hours and hours of your time over the long term so that you will not mind the effort needed up front.

Once you have created a file with processes and procedures for your business, you will want to ask that each person responsible for a particular task to audit and keep their procedural documents updated. This means that if there is a change in the process, new passwords or websites they edit and keep the document updated at all times. Why is this important? The truth is we are all vulnerable. If the individual that usually performs the task at hand needs to miss work, someone else must be able to step in and complete the project. This is a very important point. This means that even if you are a solo entrepreneur and are still running every process in your business, you should have the steps written down for all of your tasks because, let's be honest, you could easily end up in the hospital or ill. Someone might have to step in and perform some of the crucial tasks for your business. Don't let an emergency situation be the end of your business.

Some good news...

I bet as you read through the above process you might have been thinking:

1) What if I have projects with multiple people on them?
2) How can I delegate yet still be aware of a projects status and know that my business is running efficiently at all times?

I know the above questions are ones that you are asking yourself because I hear these same worries from my clients all of the time. I'm not going to sugar coat it. Delegating is difficult, and ALL entrepreneurs feel much more confident in doing so if they can take a peek into their current projects, make suggestions or corrections if needed, and stay updated at all times. Not only is this a concern for entrepreneurs, IT REALLY IS SOMETHING THAT SHOULD BE DONE. How can you possibly run a business if you don't know what is going on? After all, who will a client call if there is something they are unhappy about – YOU. Let's be real! If you don't know what's going on with your own business when a client calls, you will look very unprofessional and frankly, like an inefficient leader.

So, I said there was some good news...

Besides using the traditional checklist that I mentioned before, there are online programs and apps that you can use for your business that can 1) make the process of building your systems for your business easier, 2) let multiple people contribute to projects at one time, and 3) let you keep an eye on the status of work at all times. I will give you the names of a few such programs here, but I'd also suggest you have those who will be using these systems search the internet to find programs that work well for their needs and skill sets. The wrong program is like a pair of ill-fitting shoes – no one will use it! It will get pushed to the back of the closet. However, the right program will make your business run more efficiently, save time and even create more income because you will be able to focus on what really matters – bringing in more business.

Some Programs I've used for project and process management:

- Evernote
- Teamwork.com
- Projectmanager.com
- Basecamp.com
- Dropbox.com
- Box.com
- Project.net
- Smartsheet.com
- Myintervals.com
- Googledocs

This is by no means a complete list. New programs and apps are developed and introduced daily. Currently, these are some of the most affordable systems I know of for small business, but because new things are coming to market all of the time I suggest researching before deciding on the right system for your business. Another great way to learn about efficient online systems is to ask others in similar fields what they are currently using.

Once you have some systems in place, how do you go about delegation? As I said earlier, I understand that the idea of delegating can send many entrepreneurs over the edge. The big worry is that others will not complete the tasks as well as the owner of the business because they won't have as much buy-in or simply just won't care about the business as much as the owner does. While that may hold some truth, you need to remember as an entrepreneur that one of the reasons you've worked so hard to put systems in place is to make each task virtually mistake proof. You've also developed these systems so that clients will have no idea that your hand was not directly on the project, but that you had someone else managing it for you. I promise you that once you begin to delegate and see items in your business being completed while you are working with clients, out networking or even taking time for a little self-care you are going to fall in love with delegation.

The other bottom line is that if you don't learn to delegate and accomplish business through others, your business will top out and fizzle because you can only do so much per day.

The best way to delegate tasks in your business is to find the correct person based on skill set. Have you ever worked at a job and been handed a task to do that was too easy, too challenging or just plain boring? I know I certainly have. It made me feel undervalued, not challenged, overwhelmed and extremely frustrated. When you hire employees, you need to know exactly where their talents are, and you need to know what they really enjoy working on. How do you discover this? You ask. Looking at their resume may not always be a good indicator of their talents and best use because their previous position may not have featured any of those items. After all, they are seeking new employment for a reason. Could it be they didn't feel valued?

Once you have the right person(s) in the right position, you need to continue to ask them for feedback. Also ask them to even help you develop systems for processes as your business continues to grow. This will allow ownership of projects and create greater buy-in and loyalty to your business and brand. Employees (even contracted employees such as virtual assistants) love to feel valued and respected. Taking notice of their talents and skills and allowing them to create systems in your business is a great way to show them how much you respect their work and skill-set. Remember that positive verbal feedback always creates powerful ownership as well.

We've covered a lot in this chapter on a very critical piece of running a business successfully. The largest piece of advice I can give you on this topic is to take on the challenge of setting up systems and process in small chunks. Don't try to create all of the processes for your business at one time. Start with the most important task that you as a business owner should get off of your plate and move on to the next as you complete each one. Carefully create a list of all of the processes in your business, prioritize them in order of importance as to which should be put into a systematized process first, second and so on. Then get busy. Your processes can be as simple as a checklist that an employee would be able to reference and check off as they work or as involved as an online system or app. Be sure to keep it as simple as you can so that the process of completing the task as it is formally laid out doesn't get tossed to the back of the closet like an ill-fitting pair of shoes. Finally, be sure to ask your employees to keep all processes updated at all times. Then, if needed, someone could step into their place and take over the process with a moment's notice.

Defining your processes as described will allow you to maximize your time, and reach your financial goals while running your business like the CEO that you are. So get to work developing defined systems and creating that dream team that will allow you to fully implement and grow.

Here are some questions to ask yourself and reflect on as you get started on the process of defining systems and ultimately delegating.

What part of your business fails to get done on a regular basis but should be completed?

_____

_____

_____

What is the one task in your business that just drives you crazy? What do you just hate to do and possibly put off as a result?

_____

_____

_____

What are the simplest tasks that you could easily pass to someone right away?

_____

_____

_____

How do you feel about delegating? How could you make this process of "letting go" easier on yourself?

_____

_____

_____

Who could you go to or lean on for support or find as a mentor as you go through this process?

_____

_____

_____

Lisa Hall

Business Success Coach, Lisa Hall, started Tight Ship Business coaching in the winter of 2011. Before beginning her own coaching practice Lisa Hall was a consultant with the well-known Tony Robbins and Chet Holms organizations. Lisa developed and ran the operations department for a part of these organizations that produced marketing materials for their coaching clients. Lisa put her business success skills to good use developing systems that could effectively track business, client projects and even the inside sales team's work and the creative team's performance. Through this process and experience Lisa learned how important having organized systems are to a business by helping to take this marketing division's earning up a factor of three in just two short years.

Lisa has a degree in Human Resources and worked in the field for about a year before deciding to go back to school and earn her teaching credentials. Lisa began her career in the field of education and after fifteen years left education to pursue her own entrepreneurial dreams while beginning a business in real estate. Lisa was recognized as a top-producer after just one year with her company. When the real estate market in California declined Lisa left the business to try her hand at a couple of other businesses that eventually led her to business coaching.

Lisa Hall's background in human resources, teaching, and over 12 years of entrepreneurship, makes her a natural leader, trainer, coach and professional speaker. Lisa is a regular contributor to LinkedIn Articles, eZine online magazine and Women's Owned Business Club Magazine. Lisa is the creator of the "Business Builders Toolkit Tele-Summit and speaks at business conferences around the country. Lisa's latest endeavors include working with The University of Tennessee to bring corporate training to businesses in

Tennessee. Lisa is also developing the entrepreneurial certification program for the university.

Lisa brings experiences from her corporate positions as well as her successes and failures in her own businesses to help her clients succeed in less time and with greater profitability. Lisa helps her clients decrease the amount of time spent on their business by helping them be more productive though the use of well designed time management skills and systems. Lisa helps her clients gain more control over their business and personal lives and become more profitable in the process.

(865)308-0003

Lisa.Hall@TightShip.us

www.tightship.us

https://www.facebook.com/tightship.us?ref=hl

Twitter: @OneTightShip

Sales

CHAPTER SIX

Differentiate yourself from the competition.
Sell yourself first.
Brian K. McNeill

Have you ever thought to yourself that "Clients can get the same thing I'm selling from somewhere else?" You have heard it said often before. You must differentiate yourself from the competition. The problem is, how do we do it?

For twelve years I was a straight commission, over the road, home improvement salesperson. It seemed as if in every city where I worked, there were hundreds of companies selling the same thing I did. So how did I consistently set sales records? How did I consistently double the sales of my nearest competitor? How was I able to, on a straight commission salary, buy homes and cars and enable my wife to stay at home to raise our children?

I learned how to differentiate myself from others, and I learned how to eliminate competition. Before I reveal to you how to do this, I want you to know that before I learned these secrets, I was trapped. I was trapped in a vicious competition game of the customers always comparing my price with other companies' prices. I was always losing this battle. For you see, if you do not differentiate for your customers, they will assume that the only difference is price. Why would anyone ever choose to spend more for the exact same thing?

I was trained to differentiate our company from the competition by telling the potential customer how great our company was and about how many satisfied customers we had. We were supposed to win business by telling how long we have been in business and what a great guy the owner of our company was. The problem was that the customers that I was talking to did not seem to care about any of that, so that method failed.

I am thankful I discovered the secret to differentiating myself and eliminating competitors. I discovered the answer from two different sources, a book and a cassette.

Joe Girard was, according to the <u>Guinness Book of Records</u> the world's greatest salesperson for twelve years in a row. Joe Girard wrote a great book entitled, <u>How to</u> <u>Sell Anything to Anybody</u>. I absorbed this book. A person who didn't know any better would think that Joe Girard sold cars; but in the book, Joe revealed the secret. Joe Girard sold, according to him, the world's greatest and rarest product. Joe Girard sold Joe Girard. He sold himself so effectively that people wanted to, and very often did, buy Joe Girard. He was kind enough to throw in the car as an added benefit.

The second place I learned the secret of differentiation and elimination was from a cassette tape that I played over and over in my car. It was called "Selling You" by the late, great Napoleon Hill. Most of us know Napoleon Hill as the author of <u>Think and</u> <u>Grow Rich</u>. He also had many recordings. In my opinion, "Selling You" was one of the best.

In the recording of "Selling You" there are what Mr. Hill calls "Sales Laws." The number one Sales Law which he said should never be broken is to "Sell Yourself First"

Who are you and why should customers listen to you? This is the first question in the minds of your potential customers and clients. It must be answered, or you and what you offer are going to be just like everyone else's product with the only differentiator being price.

None of us can ever afford to have price as our only differentiator!

So, how do we do it?
Here is what I learned.
Here is what I practice.
Here is how you do it.

Step 1:

The first sale that we must make before we can work on differentiating ourselves is to ourselves.

I personally subscribe to the theory that you cannot teach a kid to ride a bicycle in a book or a classroom. We must get on the bike and pedal, so within the pages of this book, we are going to ride.
I challenge you to complete exercise # 1 before proceeding.

Exercise # 1: Set a timer for 3 minutes. In the spaces provided, write down 10 great reasons why someone should buy your product or service from you. Do this within the three minutes allotted. Once you start the clock and start writing, most people are able to quickly write down the first three or four. Then, you will have to start thinking. These first three or four answers that came to you quickly are your personal list of favorite reasons. If that is the case for you, I challenge you to press on to complete this task. People who have a challenge completing this assignment are usually overlooking the very obvious reasons as to why someone should buy what they are offering.

Note that this assignment is ten great reasons why someone should buy what you sell from you. Please do not forget to include yourself as a part of what they are buying.

GO!

TEN GREAT REASONS WHY SOMEONE SHOULD BUY WHAT I SELL FROM ME!

1.

2.

3.

4.

5.

6.

7.

8.

9.

10.

Stop the clock.

Did you finish in the allotted time?

Did you remind yourself of anything?

If you did not successfully complete this task, it means that you have either forgotten too much, or you do not yet know enough to sell what you sell. It is time for you to study again.

If you did successfully complete this exercise, congratulations! Now look back over your list. Do you like it?

There are five primary reasons why people are willing to exchange their money for what you offer.

1. Time
2. Money
3. Good Feelings
4. Good Health
5. Solutions to a Problem

Does your list of "10 Great Reasons Why Someone Should Buy What You Sell" address any of these five primary motivators to buy? Does your list address all of them? Do you need to reword some of them to make them more sellable?

Step 2: Build Your Story:

Who are you? Why are you there? What is it that is particularly redeeming about you? Are you attempting to build a great business, or are you there just to make beer money?

Do you love what you do? Can you sincerely show it? Do you love your customers? Can you demonstrate it?

You do not need to nor should you go into great detail about who you are, but the customer must know that

You are not an ax murderer

You are someone worthy of being rewarded with a sale.

Sell yourself first! Sell yourself well. Practice selling yourself. Enlist help to build your winning story.

When a client buys <u>you</u> and wants to buy you, <u>they can only get you from you</u>. They cannot get you from the competition. So they must buy you from you. The competition is a maybe, and a potential horror story. Sell you well, and you then become the safest alternative for the client. The choice becomes, buy from the known good person or risk finding another one.

By selling you, you do differentiate yourself from the competition, and you can largely eliminate them.

To help you to build your story, consider doing these exercises as well.

Exercise #1:   <u>List ten great things about yourself</u>.

1.

_____

2.

_____

3.

_____

4.

_____

5.

_____

6.

_____

7.

_____

8.

_____

9.

_____

10.

_____

Exercise # 2: <u>List ten things you have</u> <u>accomplished</u>.

1.

_____

2.

_____

3.

_____

4.

_____

5.

_____

6.

_____

7.

_____

8.

_____

9.

_____

10.

_____

Exercise # 3: <u>List ten things you want to accomplish with your current business.</u>

1.

_____

2.

_____

3.

_____

4.

_____

5.

_____

6.

_____

7.

_____

8.

_____

9.

_____

10.

_____

Brian K. McNeill

For over 21 years Brian has been engaged in the act of studying, teaching and mastering the art of professional selling.

For the first 12 of these 21 years Brian was the sales manager of a multistate Home improvement company with 17 offices. It was during those years of giving 5 motivational sales meetings a week that Brian honed his skills in selling and teaching sales.

In 1996 Brian wrote "The 22 Must Closes" 22 ways that salespeople should know how to ask for money. That publication launched Brian as an authority enabling him to share his expertise with thousands.

The responses to Brian's seminars and workshops had been universally enthusiastic and positive prompting him to open his first Sales Training Company, "Rhino Sales and Seminars" in 2006.

It is Brian's strong belief that most sales training is ineffective because it is not personalized enough. This resulted in his re-launching his company as Very Personal Sales Coaching in 2010.

Brian's Signature workshop "Ten to Win" has been requested over and over again.

tel: 1-919 345 4893
brian@verypersonalsalescoaching.com
https://www.linkedin.com/in/themostfunspeaker
https://www.facebook.com/brian.k.mcneill
https://twitter.com/BrianKMcNeill

CHAPTER SEVEN

Learn how to sell big orders to big clients.
Frank Manson

Sometimes it is often just as easy to get a large order as a small one – and the money is much better. Learn from my process of selling a million dollar's worth of air, over and over again. Selling big orders to big clients can be easy and lucrative.

A little over 6 years ago I went to see a client that I had not seen in a while, bringing a Senior Vice President from Westwood One with me on the call. My client, Scott, opened the call by producing a picture of us signing a two-year Million Dollar plus advertising contract that at the time was the largest his company or my company had ever completed. The picture had been in both of our company newsletters. While memorable and well documented, it was neither the largest or most comprehensive contract that I sold during over 30 years in Advertising, Marketing and Broadcasting.

What you do need to understand is that TV and Radio advertising falls under the category of an intangible product and actually does not involve a physical product. It is radio and TV waves sent over the air. Can you imagine the profit margin on air? For most major radio and TV outlets, it is just the labor that goes into creating the product, and the cost of sales and marketing…so it is not unusual to see 50% of the cost going direct to the bottom line.

In a career that spanned creative opportunities like bringing the NFL to the Carolinas, marketing the Jim Valvano show, and launching new pharmaceutical products, or coordinating retail promotions in 5 states for Belk or other retailers, I have had the challenge of marketing and selling really large orders to really large companies, like Anheuser Busch and GlaxoSmithKline.

I was the eager beneficiary of intensive and creative sales training courses like Dale Carnegie, Wilson Learning Systems and Miller Heiman Sales Training. I have had the opportunity, challenge and need to close million dollar plus contracts with companies-which by their very size and structure had multiple layers of purchasing and review, scenarios that Miller Heiman calls "the complex sale".

There are a number of concepts essential to understanding the methodology of selling to multiple decision makers. They include, but are not limited to "ideal customer profile", "Win/Win" selling, understanding the four or more types of buyers and understanding personal and professional wins and results.

Your Ideal Customer

If you have never attempted to determine what your company's Ideal Customer looks like, then you should address that first. In less than an hour you can assemble a group that includes yourself and either your employees or peers, or even clients, and brainstorm your way to who your ideal customer is, or should be. You should be considering the profile of your 5 best and 5 worst customers. You may be able to do this by yourself, but it helps to have a couple of other people involved to keep the conversation grounded.

Prepare a Grid like the one below with only the column labels filled in for each participant, then bring up a number of customers for discussion, including not only the biggest and best you already have on the books, but clients that you are working on, or are using a competitor. Also include clients that you have and wish you didn't, or that you have had to fire, sue or otherwise terminate the relationship.

After writing down significant characteristics of both your best and worst, then summarize the "best" comments. You'll have a map of customers you would like, and the clients to stay away from. If your prospecting pool contains more of the second type of clients, you may be "fishing in the wrong pond."

Ideal Customer Grid

Customer	Best Features of Best	Worst Features	Ideal Customer	Best Features of Worst	Worst Features
Customer A	Big Budget	Long Sales Cycle	-		
Customer B	Open Minded	Busy Schedule	-		
Customer C			—	Quick Turnaround	Slow Pay
Customer D	Annual Buys	Late for deadlines	-	—	
Customer E			-	Easy Access to Decision Makers	Many last minute changes

The Win/Win Matrix

Every Sale can be categorized in four general quadrants on this Matrix. If you want repeat sales and repeat customers, you have got to be committed to stay in the upper left hand corner, both during the sales process, the negotiation, and the completion of the sale.

	The Company Wins	TheCompany Wins	
Customer Wins	**I Win, You Win**	**I Win, You Lose**	Customer Loses
Customer Wins	**I Lose, You Win**	**I Lose, You Lose**	Customer Loses

Four Types of Buyers

The larger the order you expect to sell compared to the size of the organization you are selling to, increases the likelihood that you will have 2, 3 or 4 or more buyers involved in making the decision.

The Big Guy – also known as the President, CEO, in some cases the CFO, he or she is the person that approves or writes the check. Characteristics: Wants the bottom line. Will make the right decision for the wrong reason, and vice versa. Used to making decisions. Probably wants to grow the company.

He can "yes", when all others have said "No". Big wins for this buyer include increased sales, increased profits, lower costs, and more productivity

Your Coach – This is a person that you know well, believes in you, and would like to see your solution implemented in the customer's company. He or she probably is a company insider or top level, trusted employee.

Who Gets the Goods – Also referred to as the User Buyer. Could be a Sales Manager or Operations Manager, if you are selling a promotion involving Fresh Fruit and Vegetables to Harris Teeter, you are probably dealing with "the Cabbage Head". This person gets the benefits from what you are selling, but probably doesn't get to approve the budget.

The Rejectionist – This person can go by many names, but their job function is usually clearly defined. Does your product or service meet the standards that are required by the customer company? Names like "head of purchasing", "technical buyer", "and procurement director", "media buyer" and others. This person may also be the person that signs your contract. Win's for this person are "Safety", "keeping my job".

Once you have identified the players, three steps are next. Identify the Win's and Results for each and then decide how well you (as the sales person) have got each one covered. It helps to have someone else go through this step with you, in case you are overstating the case in either direction.

Begin tracking the sale – include all the names and relevant sales data.

Identify next step – That could be as simple as "Meet with technical buyer to talk about bid specs." Or as complex as "attend store grand opening to meet Regional Manager, and discuss spring promotion."

With this, the process begins. If your solution is expensive, or affects multiple layers in the customer's organization, the more layers of decision-making and opinion will need attention. The smaller the budget and project, the fewer people will be involved. Sometimes it's very important to close a small piece of business to get included in the vendor list, with the idea of pitching the big idea in the future.

How long is this sales cycle? In most of my businesses, the average was around 14 months, and I tracked it. I have a friend that sold naval communications equipment and systems to the military, with a 2 to 5 year sales cycle.

There are excellent resources cited below:
1. Strategic Selling, Robert E. Miller and Stephen E. Heiman
2. The New Strategic Selling, Stephen E. Heiman and Diane Sanchez
3. Conceptual Selling, Robert E. Miller, Stephen E. Heiman and Tad Tujela.

Frank Manson

From "the Cowardly Lion" in the Wizard of Oz, to morning show host, North Carolina Sportscaster of the Year, and volunteer awards from the Advertising community, the Boy Scouts and the Governor of North Carolina, to closing multi-million dollar advertising accounts, Frank Manson's professional and public service careers have included a wide variety of leadership roles, and opportunities to help organizations take great leaps forward.

A writing career that started in high school, as editor of Granby High School's "Spectator", he led the student staff to a Medalist Award from the Columbia Scholastic Press Association. On stage, from Charlie's Aunt, Gypsy, Plaza Suite, the Crucible to the Odd Couple are just some of the productions he has brought to life from school to Little Theatre.

In two years, Frank once spoke to over 70 Rotary Clubs, as a part of the Rotary Group Study Exchange Award. 35 of those were during 45 days in Tasmania, Australia.

His career has included Capitol Broadcasting, as General Sales Manager for over 14 radio networks. He has been an Entrepreneur, merging two small companies that were in debt and losing money, into broadcasting and advertising firm that he ultimately sold to Westwood One.

Frank has written, produced and been the talent for thousands of Radio and TV commercials. Other activities include: United Way President, 16 years as a CASL youth soccer coach, Silver Beaver and Scoutmaster of the Year awards from the Boy Scouts, plus some success at tennis and golf.

Frank is a Registered Representative with Triangle Financial Services, Guardian Life Insurance and Park Avenue Securities. His practice includes Individuals developing their retirement and long term care plans while protecting their families and assets. One area of particular focus is assisting high tech companies with their active business needs. His background includes Business Consulting, and he was a Regional Vice President for Westwood One, a leading provider of analog and digital content, to the broadcast and on-line sectors. His work spans diverse areas such as Cloud Based software, NASCAR , the NFL and many small businesses. In addition, Frank teams with other financial professionals and specialists to collectively solve and identify solutions to complex issues that potentially can affect your financial future and Business continuation. He has a B.A. in Political Science from N.C. State University.

Frank and his wife Violet have lived in the Triangle for over 20 years, and have 3 children, Albert, Gillian and Andrew.

Contact: fmanson@financialguide.com

919.414.4717

www.linkedin.com/pub/frank-manson/2/3b/321

CHAPTER EIGHT

Implement the secret to referral based growth.
Tim Pedersen

Ask for referrals. Utilize and activate your network to create more business growth.

Within your niche, your successful clients will have amassed a power sphere of like individuals who would benefit from your services as well. Ask for introductions or create a webinar to add value to their meetings. Make the referrer look good in everything you do in order to create a welcomed and repeated process. Create a package offering to encourage group buy-in.

You can utilize and activate your network to create business! You spent a lot of time acquiring your top clients – or at least making sure they stay your top clients. As a business owner, a key word for success is leverage. How can you leverage the work that you have put into a great client to acquire more clients like them or in their same niche? One thing that often happens in the business process is that we sell, sell, sell and then do, do, do. We spend a great amount of time working on who to target and then on actually selling or acquiring them as clients. Easing the sell process can make it a more continuous source, lessening the dips between the Sell and the Do.

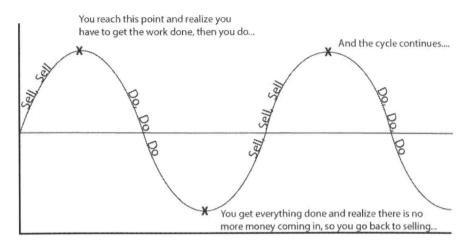

The idea first was actually brought to me by a client many years ago. It was a large law firm that worked with a lot of smaller firms for cases around the country. The marketing director for the firm asked me if I minded if he passed on my name to another law firm that admired the work that we have been doing for them. It seemed like a silly question to ask me. Of course I would appreciate referrals to other companies! That is when the light turned on, and I realized I could ask for these referrals from clients. Over the years, I've learned some things along the way that have helped to streamline the process and make it very profitable. There are a lot of ways to approach this, but throwing it out into the air and seeing if referrals come in tends to not work. Asking the right clients, approaching it the right way; and even giving a little coaching to be sure you are presented in the best light, can make a world of difference.

Coaching your referral partners.

This may sound a bit controlling or even rude. Why would you want to jeopardize getting referrals by trying to control the conversation?

First, I wouldn't look at it as control as much as it is a guide or framework for your referrer to have when going out into his or her network to refer you. The last thing you want them to do is tell the potential new client how cheap you are, or how they can call you at 9 p.m. or on the weekend, and you will answer the phone. These may be actions that you are happy to provide for them, but may not be something that you would do for every single client. A little guidance will go a long way and can easily be done by treating them to a lunch and having the conversation with them. Feel free to create a cheat sheet of information for them or even a little packet. This is also a good time to take a long hard look at the type of client you are trying to attract. Be sure the information and focus that you portray to your referrer is in line with that, and that they understand it.

There are a few ways that you could set up that these referrals take place. Let's take a look at a few...

The Pass Along

Well meaning referrers will usually start with the offer to pass along your information to other companies. Although this sounds flattering and exciting at first, it is doomed from the beginning. We all know the average sale takes 5-9 touches to happen. Touches can be in the form of brand recognition, phone call, direct mail, letter, referral, etc. The passing of information is not coming from a hired sales person, but a well-meaning client. The scenario where this happens is completely out of your control in this. It may be your next big client, but because the referral was introduced at the wrong time or without the right connection or value proposition, it could be dead in the water. Because you have no information about the company to whom you were referred, you are sitting next to the phone waiting for this mystery company to call. It may never happen!

The Hand Off

This is simply the Pass Along with the added caveat that you also are getting the information provided to you about the other company and who the contact person should be. This could happen in the form of an email in which both of you are introduced. Or it may be THE email that introduces you or a follow up from the referrer. It may look something like this:

Susan,

It was great to see you at lunch today. I wanted to follow up on our conversation regarding the company I told you about. The person you need to talk to is George. He is a great guy, and I am not just saying that because he is CCd here! I have attached his contact information for you, and I fully believe he can get you over that hurdle you mentioned.

I just ask that you don't keep him so busy that he doesn't have the time to work on my account!

George - Susan is the great colleague that I mentioned to you that I have known through networking for many years. I trust that you will treat her and her company with the spark that you have brought to the table for me all these years. With Susan's permission, I have added her contact information here as well.

Best regards,

With the Hand Off, you now have the needed information to move forward with this hot referral. The stage has been set that you can follow up with an email or call. Be sure to provide Susan with your value proposition and delve into the hurdle that was mentioned. At this point, you are on your way to creating Susan as your next client. But your job is not done yet.

Be sure to follow up with the referrer to let them know how it went. Over a casual lunch or conversation, you could review the process with them. Be open about what was working. Be positive and grateful. Create an experience so that the referrer feels excited about creating again for you - hopefully again and again! This positive feedback should create a conversation that will strengthen the relationship with your referrer and give them the knowledge to bring you more and more potential clients.

The Win/Win

I love the win/win scenario. In this situation, you are directly creating value for the referral source while value is being created for you. This situation works well when the referral source markets or has clients that could also use your services. For instance, a printer that markets to small businesses could be a good referral source to business coaches, marketers, SEO specialists, social media companies, and so on. So how do you create the win/win? Offer to create an event or "offer" for the referral source. This could be a webinar, seminar, discount, lunch and learn or a Google hangout. Ideally, the referral source is the host and introduces you. The overall purpose of the event is that the host is dedicated to the success of his/her client. They are having you present as a way focus on that. Your job as the presenter is to create value and do your best to compliment and make the host look good. Create that special offer and incentive for the attendees. Additionally, offer follow up sessions for the attendees. Have dates ready to present, so attendees can sign up during the event.

If a live presentation does not work, the introduction or offer could always be done through email, flyers, brochures, or mailed out with invoices or statements.

The important thing to remember here is the value of the content you are providing. It has to be a presentation where you give incredible value. It cannot be a sales presentation. Typically, it will be understood that the last few minutes may be you giving information on your company and how you can solve the problem you just presented. But if the whole experience was a sales process, you will not only make the host look bad, but will damage the relationship as well. I just listened to a webinar during which the presenter did a great job in setting up the "sale" at the end. He was up front in stating that it was an hour long presentation. For 50 minutes he gave it all that he had and was committed to creating value for the attendees. In the last ten minutes, he described what his company did and presented an incredible offer that he had put together with the host. This allows for an authentic presentation where the goals are clearly stated at the onset. It also created some excitement as I was looking forward to this great offer!

Compensation

This can be a tricky subject to approach, but occasionally, some form of compensation is mentioned or expected. There are a couple of ways that this can be done. If you are dealing with someone who is in a sales position, you may set up a referral bonus or fee for them that can be based on a percentage of the initial sale. You could also create a percentage of recurring sales if your product or service is repeated by the client. If they are a business owner, the offer of additional services can be a welcomed compensation for their efforts helping you. Delivering a little extra work for them for their efforts might be enough of an incentive. If you are working with someone that you have helped substantially to grow their business, the only compensation they may want is to know that they are helping you to grow to your business.

Here are a few ways to get started with your analysis of your clients so that you can turn them into valued referral partners. Create a list of your best clients. This may be a short list; or if you are lucky, a long one.

Consider the relationship you have with each client. Rate it between 1 and 10. (Ten could mean that your relationship is flawless and open; one could mean that there is lots of work to be done to create a good relationship.)

Consider their reach into their community and rate that from 1-10. Ten could mean they are a connector and are well known in the networking circles.

Think about the industry they are in, and whether you want to delve deeper into that particular industry. Ten could mean "very much so."

Consider whether you have made a difference for this client so that your service to them becomes an example to show other like businesses. Ten would mean that you have made a considerable difference to the client.

Consider the financial impact of each individual sale for the client. A single "sale" for an attorney might rate a ten, but an individual sale for a dry cleaner would tend to be a 1.

Do this for each of your clients, and it will become clear who you should have conversations with. Also, it will create a path for those clients whom you might want to focus on.

Use the chart below to develop a visual analysis of the rating system for clients who are referral partners.

CLIENT	Relationship	Community Reach	Differences Made w/ Client	Score

Asking for referrals is not a daunting task or one that has to be looked on as a chore, it is a great way to build a deeper relationship with a client that you appreciate. It may easily encourage the client to help you. It is an excellent way to start creating an expertise and presence in a niche to promote your expertise. Fill out the chart. Look at the numbers. See how you can double your business by asking for referrals!

Tim Pedersen

Branding consultant and creative director, Tim Pedersen, has been a keeper of the brand for over 25 years. An early understanding and love for the affect that great design and brand strategy can have on a product or service became the catalyst for this devoted direction.

Tim began his career in publication design, working for jazz and food magazines. The fast paced world of monthly design demands wasn't enough for his veracious appetite for design, so he also created advertising departments within the publications to not only create additional profit centers within the corporations, but to create an additional creative outlet.

This eventually evolved into his first company, Function Media, then to Pedersen Design and his now teen baby – Right Brain Branding. As "keepers of the brand" Right Brain often becomes an extension of large corporation's marketing departments – working on brainstorming, strategy and implementation.

Being a small business and loving how small businesses can harness the power of the web to create a global presence, Tim and Right Brain Branding often work with smaller companies in creating their 5 year branding plan (what do they want to be when they grow up) and creating the creative path to get there. As tools and technologies emerge to assist in this process, Right Brain is there to evaluate and add to the marketing mix when applicable. Currently, the benefit for a small business of engaging Right Brain Branding is the full spectrum of implementation that can be provided – from web development, logo and identity creation, SEO, local marketing, collateral, advertising design and more. This keeps the business owner focused on the business and Right Brain on the creative marketing.

Tim is a husband and a father to 3 children - one in college, one in high school and one in elementary school. Since moving from Miami, his family has grown to include 2 horses, 2 dogs, 2 cats and a flock of chickens. If he is not working in the yard, you will find him at Crossfit or a home improvement store.
You can connect with him at LinkedIn at www.linkedin.com/in/rightbraintim/ or at www.RightBrainBranding.com

Marketing

CHAPTER NINE

Apply the secret of marketing: simplicity.
Diana M. Needham

Keep your marketing activities simple. Choose just 3 effective activities that put you in front of your ideal customer every week and be consistent. Focus is the key to success.

"Three Rules of Work: Out of clutter find simplicity; From discord find harmony; In the middle of difficulty lies opportunity." Albert Einstein

Clearly marketing is not a new idea for entrepreneurs. There are literally thousands of books and resources offering valuable information on this topic. Yet marketing remains an area that eludes the majority of entrepreneurs. Many view marketing as not only expensive but also complicated.

As an entrepreneur, one of the top priorities is marketing your business so that profits increase, revenues grow, and you can have a bigger impact on both your community and the world. You started this business because you have a solution to a problem people have and your solution makes a difference in people's lives.

If you are like many entrepreneurs, you may be struggling with how to market your business to attract your ideal clients and customers.

How do I know? Many of my clients love what they do, but hate the marketing aspects.

Many are tired of all the conflicting marketing advice everywhere they turn. Their inboxes are flooded with the latest and greatest marketing ideas (everything from make money in our sleep using Facebook ads to creating eye-popping video to traditional article and content marketing).

Most feel overwhelmed and confused about all the options. Some have tried lots of them, only to give up from the stress of trying to do it all. They suffer from exhaustion, and investments of time and money with few tangible results.

It doesn't have to be that way.

Read on to learn how you can simplify your marketing efforts to just 3 strategies and get the results you want.

First, let's end the definition confusion.

The word "marketing" means different things to different people, with some differentiating between advertising, public relations, promotions and sales, which all fall under the broad umbrella of "marketing". To keep it simple for the purposes of this tip, marketing is the process by which a product or service is introduced and promoted to potential customers.

Without effective marketing, your business may offer the best products or services in your industry, but **none** of your potential customers will know about it. Simply stated, marketing's job is to understand what the customer wants and needs, and then to provide it.

Whether you are selling a product or a service, one of the critical skills is marketing. The truth is our number one focus is marketing, **not** delivering the product or service we offer. Without effective marketing that gets results, revenue trickles in at best.

To avoid the overwhelming choices and confusion, pick just 3 simple marketing strategies that put you in front of your ideal client or customer and be consistent with those 3. Without a clear strategy and implementation plan, your marketing efforts will fail.

Here are the 4 simple steps for figuring out those top 3 strategies for focus.

Step 1: Identify your ideal client or customer, in as much detail as you can.

The first step in marketing is knowing **specifically** who you are looking for. Who you are called to serve that will pay for the solution you have?

Remember that customer you had who was just perfect? You know, the one who, if you had 10 just like her, your business would be thriving?

See that person and give her a name. Instead of seeing your market as a sea of nameless faces, identify one person you know, and wrap all your marketing messages and activities around her.

Write down all the details about her here.

Ideal client characteristic	Answer	Comments
Age		
Marital status		
Kids? If so, add the ages in the comments section		
Other details (education level, interests, hobbies, -What is important to her, values, etc.)		
What challenges are keeping her awake at 3 AM that you solve…and she will pay for that solution?		

Remember the purpose of being in business is to make money, so your ideal clients <u>must</u> have a burning challenge they will pay to solve.

Step 2: Figure out where she is spending time, both online and offline. Now that we know **who** we are looking for, the next step is identifying **where** she is spending time.

95+% of all business owners are looking for clients in their local market, even if a large portion of their sales come from online methods.

Where is your ideal client congregating locally?

What organizations, groups, clubs, or charity organizations is she part of? Ask yourself how you can plug into those groups and organizations.

Where is she spending time online? Which social media sites is she using? What blogs is she reading? Who is she following for advice and insights?

A big word of caution: The shiny social media syndrome may be killing your business!

Social media is more beneficial for gaining visibility and building relationships over time. It is a longer term strategy, so if you are just starting out, it is best to invest your time in offline activities, where you will see faster results.

The focus and demographics for the top social media sites are very different. Leveraging social media requires time, effort, and focus and can be a huge time waster unless you have a solid strategy and are clear on how to reach your ideal client or customer on each of the platforms selected.

Because social media is such a hot topic, information about the top 3 sites is outlined below for your review. Of course there are many others (You Tube, Google +, Pinterest, etc.) but these are the top 3.

Facebook is the number one social media website on the Internet. Facebook has more than 1 billion active users; these users spend one-third of their Internet time on the site, with roughly half visiting the site every day. This equates to people spending about 500 billion minutes per month on Facebook. Each user averages over 15 hours per month on the site.

The top three reasons people connect with a **brand** on Facebook is: (1) To learn about new products (35%); (2) To receive coupons and discount offers (37%); (3) To advise people they know what products/services they support (41%).

If your business is direct to consumer (rather than business to business), and your ideal client spends time here, this may be a platform to consider, once your business is established and you have revenue coming in.

In order to have your business in front of your ideal clients, you'll need to invest in ads. This requires either an outside resource to create and manage your strategy or your investment of time to learn it. Ask yourself if this is the best use of time.

Twitter has more than 550 million accounts, with 141.8 million in the U.S., according to Semiocast (7/30/12).

The most interesting thing about Twitter is that it limits what you have to say or share, which is known as a "Tweet," to 140 characters—not 140 letters, 140 total characters, including spaces and punctuation. In other words, it keeps to the "KISS" rule, Keep it Short and Simple.

For businesses, Twitter may be an effective way to share quick snippets of information, like a promotion or quick tip.

LinkedIn is the premier professional network and has 300 million members across 200 countries. LinkedIn focuses more on professional and business networking than either Facebook or Twitter. Since the average income of the professional on LinkedIn is $109K, if your market is professionals, - –be sure to have a robust presence on this platform. Read more in our tip about leveraging LinkedIn here. (link to that chapter)

Step 3: Get in front of your ideal client so she knows not only who you are, but the solution you provide.

How do you do that? Go back to your list of places she spends time.

Where can you go to network with your ideal clients?

Which groups or organizations can you visit to confirm she is there?

Does it make sense to invest time, money, and energy in these groups?

Where can you go to give a talk? Having a great presentation that provides high value to your ideal client is one of the top strategies for building your business. Make sure you have a call to action at the end, and lead the participants to opt in for your free report, audio, or video.

The goal is to move your ideal clients to your email list so you can expand on the relationship you are building by speaking to them. Having a follow up strategy in place is critical.

Identify just 3 marketing strategies and be diligent about taking action every week.

Capture the selected 3 marketing strategies, the actions required to make each one work, and the activities you will do this week to move your business forward.

My top 3 marketing strategies	Actions required to make this work	Activities this week

Wrapping this up

The final step is tracking your results, so that you know what activities to keep doing and which to discontinue.

Here is one way to do it. Capture your strategies, key activities, and results below.

Marketing Strategies (month)	Key activities performed (what exactly did you do this month)	Results (leads, clients, referrals, partners, etc.)

Most of us never make the time to analyze what is working and what is not working. You'll be surprised at what you learn from this activity.

For example, list "Networking" as one key strategy and list all the networking meetings you attend. Be honest about the results you have seen this month from each one.

It will become crystal clear which ones to continue and which ones to gracefully exit. It makes no business sense to invest more time in specific networking groups where your ideal client is either not present or not interested (unless your income is such that engaging purely for social reasons is your choice).

Track how many ideal prospects you meet every week. How many agree to a follow up conversation where you can actively listen, present your solution, and ask the prospect to work with you?

By having clearly defined marketing strategies in place and tracking to gauge results the stress and confusion will soon fade away. You might even decide you enjoy marketing!!

Stay focused on what works, keep it simple to implement, and watch your business soar!

A Real World Case Study

How a local message therapist went from just a handful of clients to 400 and gained a 3500% increase in her business in 60 days.

Let me show you how following this simple marketing formula totally transformed a local business a few summers ago.

When Karen, a lovely massage therapist, and I met, she was in overwhelm, confusion, and exhaustion. She was working a 3-day a week job she hated because, quite frankly, she needed the income to keep the lights on while she was trying to keep her massage business going. She honestly had no idea how to market her business, and her head hurt from trying to figure it out.

What she had was a big dream for her business and her life. She knew exactly what she wanted: a set number of hours per week running her massage business full time, to not be working for the chiropractor 3 days a week, time for her hobbies and family, and relief from the financial stress she felt every single day.

When I asked her, what do you need right now to move forward toward making that dream be a reality?

Her response was: "I need to see the path". Although she knew what she wanted, she could not see how to get there.

Starting with what she had, I put together a simple plan for her to move forward. We used the simple steps outlined in this chapter to make it happen.

We started where she was.

When we began, she had 3 things: a web site that looked like all the other massage therapists in the area, a Facebook page with 11 likes, and a LinkedIn profile that had an outdated picture.

We clearly defined who her ideal client is and gave her a name. This woman is over 40, stressed, and has physical pain. We gathered all the information we could about her.

Next we figured out where this ideal client was, both offline and online.

For fastest results, we invested almost no time on social medial. (Remember social media is a longer term strategy, and we needed cash fast.)

Karen was doing some local networking that was yielding a few results, so we kept that.

We knew this ideal client was looking online when she needed a massage therapist so we focused our efforts there.

We put in place just a few marketing strategies
to get in front of this ideal client.

The biggest issue was that Karen's business could not be found online, unless you happened to have her specific web site address. She was nowhere to be found when someone was searching for "massage therapist, her town" (which is how most of us search for the things we are looking for online).

We created 2 simple videos (with the call to action to call her to book an appointment) and placed her business strategically on the search engines, specific online directories, one wellness site, and review sites.

Karen asked her top clients to write reviews on specific review sites, so we could gather social proof that she delivers a high quality service and customer experience.

We tracked results.

Within a week of putting these first pieces into place, Karen doubled the number of massages she gave and almost doubled her income over the previous week.

By carefully tracking her presence online, I saw a rise daily. We celebrated when her site and videos began to show up on the Google map and first 2 pages of the search results for massage therapist in her town. This happened within a few weeks.

As soon as Karen gained some momentum, her dream of having a full time business in her massage practice came true. She left the job with the chiropractor in August, **just a month** after we started putting these simple marketing strategies in place.

What happened next took both of us by surprise.

The previous year Karen had contacted Living Social to ask them to run a special massage deal for her. They refused, since she had no real online presence, and they could not validate her service online via reviews.

Now they were calling her, asking her to run a deal! She sold **400 massages in 3 ½ days**! Even after Living Social took their percentage, this was a real cash windfall for her.

This situation created another challenge. Karen's business is a one-woman show, so how was she going to deliver 400 massages?

Not everyone showed up at once, which was a blessing.

She brought in 2 of the message therapists from her massage training programs to help. She maintained close contact with every new client who came in.

As clients experienced Karen's caring and healing approach, they began to ask if she could see their spouses, family members, and friends who were in pain or had stress-related problems. This word of mouth marketing is priceless!

Over Christmas last year, Karen sold 40 gift certificates with **no advertising**. Her clients love her and want to share her healing gifts with their friends and family members.

New opportunities are coming her way, and even I have to wait for an appointment!

Karen saw in just a few short months a 3500% increase in her business.

How did all that happen? We cleared away all the marketing clutter and created a path forward that was simple and highly effective at getting her more clients and profits.

We leveraged simple marketing strategies and followed a marketing plan with timelines.

She provided great customer service and connected with her community and clients.

So you might be thinking "Great for Karen, but that's not possible for me." Let me share a few more things about Karen.

- She was 63 years old when we started the project.
- She had invested $25K to secure her massage training. This massage business **is** her retirement plan.
- While she is very gifted in what she does, she knew nothing about the technologies and marketing processes needed to move her business forward.

If she can do it, you can do it!

Just follow the steps covered in this chapter, avoid the "bright shiny object syndrome" and focus on actions that yield results!

Diana M. Needham

Best-selling author, speaker, and marketing strategist, Diana M. Needham, started Needham Business Consulting in 2008 following a 26 year term in the corporate world as Director and Vice President at JP Morgan Chase. During those years Diana honed her leadership, communication, and business skills by refining banking processes and systems for performance and leading strategy teams. Now she has taken her experience to the street, focusing on sharing simple marketing systems for business growth to authors, speakers, and consultants.

Similar to the refinement of banking processes, Diana now leverages her planning, communication, and implementation skills, working closely with clients to streamline their businesses, step by step, and serves as a mentor and advocate for their success. She works with authors, speakers, and consultants to map out what Diana calls their 'fastest (simplest) path to cash.' I'm always planning marketing strategies from the perspective of asking: What is the fastest way for my clients to get in front of their ideal clients and to grow their visibility and expert status?"

Diana explains, "What I have discovered by working with hundreds of entrepreneurs is that we tend to make things more complicated than they need to be. I am all about keeping it simple to take action, actually implement, and get real results (more profits, more income, and more clients). I help authors, speakers, and consultants who are frustrated, overwhelmed, and stressed, to determine how to market their businesses and map out their 'fastest path to cash.' Being highly visible to their market is a critical key to success."

Diana is mother of two adult children and has one grand dog and two grand cats. She loves fitness, yoga, meditation, personal development, and hanging out with entrepreneurial friends on Facebook and LinkedIn.

For more information and to connect with Diana Needham on LinkedIn visit: www.linkedin.com/in/dianamneedham/. Learn more about Needham Business Consulting at: http://dianamneedham.com/.

CHAPTER TEN

**Turn your networking and 1-on-1's into a
sustainable system of lead generation.
Christine Clifton**

Invite like-minded business owners into a conversation with you and manage it just like you would hold a meeting: it has a beginning (get to know them/their needs); a middle (tell them about you and what you're looking for); and an end (connect them to a resource or invite them to refer/hire you). Using this process will fill your sales funnel fast!

Most business owners never look at the return on their marketing investments. They often spontaneously toss money at something some marketing expert said they ought to do. They twitch this way and do their website-; they twitch that way and do social media, and they twitch that way and create a brochure or place an ad. I lovingly call this "spastic marketing".

Even if they do look at their return on investment, business owners typically only look at the return on (money) investment, or ROI. One of the most overlooked (and valuable!) resources we business owners have is TIME – and many 'spend' it without much thought of what return they gain from it. I call this Return On Time Investment or ROTI.

One of the biggest 'wastes' of time I see in face-to-face marketing is the time spent networking and in 1-on-1's. In networking, there are those people who come in, deal out their business cards like a poker hand, and then move on to the next group. There are others that come in and hang out on the perimeter, seemingly uncertain about how to go about this whole thing called networking. Then there are those of us who have some great conversations, but don't see much coming from it.

I say that 1-on-1's are a lot like bad dating. We like someone; set up a time to meet; have a pleasant chat; and then we both leave, wondering what is going to happen next.

If you're laughing right now, then you've likely experienced a bit of this. I have, too. When I started my business, I enthusiastically began networking anywhere I could find. I joined a women business owners group. I went to regular networking events as often as I could, and I became a sought-after local speaker in another group.

At the end of one particular year in business, I looked back and asked myself "What are you getting from all of this activity?" The answer was "Not much." Sure, I made a lot of great connections, met some wonderful people, and got to teach, which I loved. But my ROTI was dismal. I knew I needed to start doing things differently.

When you don't have a concerted approach towards where you're spending your marketing time, you end up wasting a lot of it. You're going to all of these meetings, yet you either aren't meeting the right people, or your messaging isn't compelling enough to draw the right people to you. You're having a bunch of 1-on-1's, but they just seem to fizzle out for some reason. All of this time adds up quickly to lost money.

Maybe you've tried a system that worked for someone else. Or maybe you're part of a coaching group that taught you to do things their way. Or perhaps you're networking, –but you don't really like it. Or you're speaking, and you don't really like that. You've bounced from thing to thing, -but nothing seems to work really well for you.

If you're currently networking and having 1-on-1s – and they aren't working well for you right now – the good news is that, with a few small tweaks, you will likely begin finally seeing results.

There are a few key things that you need to ask yourself first:

Am I going to the right places to network? Are your ideal clients there? Can they connect you to your ideal client? Do you even know who your ideal client is? If you don't, that's the place to start and then examine if you're going to the right events.

Do I like to network? Are you like me and a little on the quiet side or introverted? Do you enjoy working a room and meeting a lot of people? If you don't, then networking may not be the ideal marketing activity for you – or you might need to shift your mindset or expectations of networking.

How comfortable am I 'selling' myself? Are you a little hesitant to tell people that you think you can help them? Would you prefer them to show interest in talking to you first? If you don't feel confident telling someone that you're the solution to their problem, then you probably need some selling skills training.

Once you've moved through those questions, here is how you can shift your current in-person activities so they're more fruitful for you:

1.Time-block your week to hold 1-on-1's – Set aside blocks of time every week to schedule 1-on-1's. They can be phone chats or in-person chats or a mix of both. You can use a system like TimeTrade to make it easy to book phone chats. Find a local coffee shop or restaurant, and set it up so that you meet with several people in a row. This process makes it easy for you to structure your other business activities around these established conversation times – instead of constantly scrambling to find a good time to meet with someone.

2.When networking, invite people to have a conversation – Once you've set up your system, you know the time available in your schedule. As you're networking and you meet a kindred spirit, you can now easily bridge them into having a conversation with you –

either in-person or over the phone. It happens in the moment, when it's most natural. This approach is much better than getting home and staring at a stack of business cards and not knowing where to start.

3.Turn your conversations into a "mini-meeting" – There is a beginning, middle, and end to every conversation. As you enter into one, keep in mind that you want to hold it in three parts: a) Ask about them and their needs; b) Tell them about you and your needs; c) Connect them to a resource. This structure holds true for both networking and 1-on-1's. In networking, it enables you both to move on to chat with other people and they are expecting your follow-up. In 1-on-1's, this process makes the conversation fruitful for both of you and gives you a natural reason to follow-up.

Here's how these systems can (legally!) double your income with a healthy ROTI:

	D	**B**	**A**	**C**
Invitations:	**6**	6	**4**	4
Conversion:	**75%**	50%	**50%**	75%
New Clients:	**4.5**	3	**2**	3

Looking at Example A as our baseline: You invite 4 people to talk to you about what you do. You're successful in converting half of them to a new client. You've gained – two new clients.

Example B: You've gotten better at the invitation, so you now invite 6 people to talk to you about what you do. You're doing the same with your conversions at 50%. You've gained 3 new clients, which is a 50% INCREASE. (Not bad, huh?)

Example C: You still only invited 4 people to talk to you about what you do. You've improved your conversion rate to 75%. You've gained 3 new clients, which is a 50% INCREASE. (Pretty good, right?)

Example D: You've gotten better at the invitation, so you invite 6 people to talk to you about what you do. You've improved your conversion rate to 75%. You've gained 4.5 new clients (just work with me, here!), which is a 125% INCREASE. (Holy cow!)

Look at that! You've more than doubled your new client growth by getting better at both your invitation and your conversation conversion.

When you take the time to ensure you're going to the right networking events where your targeted clients are, you have a greater chance of meeting potential new clients. Having now time-blocked your week, it makes it easy to bridge those you meet networking into a private conversation with you. That personal conversation is where the relationship building begins because you're looking for an opportunity to HELP them, not necessarily to SELL them.

When they know you're looking to help them, they relax and often naturally want to help you in return. Whether you're connecting them to a book, a colleague, a networking group, or to your own services, they are more open to the suggestion after you've had this personal interaction with them.

Here's my suggested action plan for you:

1.Ideal client profile – If you don't have one, begin developing a profile for your ideal client. List demographics – like gender, age range, industry - as well as psychographics – like mindset, interests, attitudes - in order to paint a full picture of who you really want to work with.

2.Networking assessment – Go back and look at the groups you've been active in and really discern whether it is the right group for you to be spending your time. Now that you've got your ideal client profile, what other groups might be more worth your time?

3.Marketing activity assessment – Looking at the activities you're a part of, ask yourself what training you might need to improve your results. It might be sales training or public speaking. Be sure that you're leveraging your strengths by choosing the marketing activities aligned with you and your business.

4.<u>Resource library</u> – Take some time to make a list of the resources that you can provide to those you're meeting. It may be a ready-list of the members of your referrals group; or it might be a word document of your favorite business books-.. It might even be a piece of your marketing materials.

When I took that long, hard look at how I was spending my time, I made all of these changes to my approach over time. As I did, I began feeling a sense of calm about my schedule. Creating that container of time to schedule people into gave my mind the freedom to focus more on my business strategy. This approach also reduced my email inbox volume significantly because there was very little "back and forth" trying to find a time that worked for both of us.

I began to get hired by people by the end of my 1-on1's with them, without selling them on anything. I simply asked them questions and offered some suggestions or resources – and they were so impressed that they hired me right then and there. My conversion rate used to be around 20% and, today, is around 90%. This growth is because of the 3-step meeting approach and because my 1-on-1's are with more of my ideal potential clients. I'm actually now having fewer 1-on-1's and earning more income than before.

Using compelling messaging adds to my success because I know my ideal client so well that I say things about my work that they really want and need. The client stories that I choose to tell them are also part of what helps them make a decision. The key to your success is to purposefully implement these processes over time so you, too, can see your ROTI grow.

Christine Clifton

Christine Clifton is a surThriver: a southern woman living in a northern land; the only girl in a family full of boys; an articulate and social introvert; and a practical spiritualist. She never really felt like she fit in, yet she tried to – her whole life. Though she was highly successful in her 20 year corporate career, she suffered half of those years with chronic fatigue and fibromyalgia – that was a sure sign that something didn't quite fit.

She's now well-traveled on her path of entrepreneurship and has found health and a true purpose that fits: holding the space for the person to come forth more naturally into their work and into their service to their community. She has a special gift of teaching people soft skills and specific processes to be heard and make a bigger impact in their lives and work.

Mindful and creative-thinking people hold a special place in her practice, in part, because she is one. She understands the overwhelm and energy drain of the demands of business today and She can help them navigate it well.

Christine Clifton helps mindful service entrepreneurs and corporate professionals *Say what they need to Say, so they can Get where they want to Go, and Earn what they're Worth.* She draws forth their natural strengths so they speak from a place of conviction and connect with the right people easily. After working with her, they see their own value, find their own voice, and present themselves confidently.

Christine also helps business teams get more done and have more fun. She helps them see how their role plays a part in the company vision as well as within the team itself which increases collaboration. As a result, the team relates with each other better and productivity and morale grows.

With 20 years of corporate experience in Management, Human Resources, Operations, and Sales – and more than 6 years of entrepreneurship – Christine understands the demands of business today. She knows the secret to being heard in today's dynamic business environment: *you must connect personally and powerfully with others.* In order to do so, you must leverage your self-awareness and take the time to understand the people around you. Only then can you speak in ways they will hear.

In addition to her multi-faceted business experience, Christine is a former Senior Professional in Human Resources and she graduated from Coach U. She holds an undergraduate in Business Administration with a Management emphasis and earned a Master of Business Administration with a Marketing specialty. Her background is wonderfully harmonized in practical business and human behavior – as well as corporate and entrepreneurship.

Christine is the author of her newly published guidebook "Your Spirit at Work: Bring more of You through what you Do so your vision comes True." She supports, first, the person and their aspirations, and then helps them bring more of their natural selves through the work that they do. As The Business Conversation Expert, Christine believes that the world is cheated if you don't bring your unique voice into it. She is a coach, trainer, author and speaker dedicated to helping people have mindful business conversations so they can make a bigger impact.

You can connect with Christine at
www.MindfulBusinessMatters.com, or LinkedIn at
www.linkedin.com/in/cclifton/, or Twitter at @NoShoutStandOut, or
Facebook at http://www.facebook.com/MindfulBusinessMatters .

Or you can reach out the old-fashioned way via email Christine@MindfulBusinessMatters.com or phone 201-738-7463.

Special Bonus from Diana, Earl, and Marie

Now that you have your copy of *17 Legal Ways to Double Your Income*, you are on your way to growing your business fast! Just pick one of the ways that resonates with you and take action to implement. Don't allow yourself to become overwhelmed by all 17! Just pick one and get moving.

You'll also receive the special bonus we created to provide another big dose of business inspiration ... Diana's *30-minute interview with Larry Winget*, filled with wisdom and insights about marketing your business and Larry's 3 Rules of Business. You'll receive access to not only the audio but the written transcript.

Not sure who Larry Winget is? He is a six-time *New York Times/Wall Street Journal* bestselling author and a member of the International Speaker Hall Of Fame. He has starred in his own television series and appeared in national television commercials. Larry is also a regular contributor on many news shows on the topics of money, personal success, parenting and business. Larry is also the trademarked **Pitbull of Personal Development®.**

While this interview is offered for sale, as a special bonus you can claim it for free here:

http://17LegalWaysToDoubleYourIncome.com/bookbonus/

We are in your corner. Let us know how we can help you further. Here's to doubling your income...fast!

Best,

Diana, Earl, and Marie

CHAPTER ELEVEN

Make a perfect business impression.
Marie Snider

Create and rehearse a compelling thirty second "elevator speech". A compelling "elevator speech" will make you stand out from the crowd. Clarifying your target audience will enable those listening to make effective referrals to your business.

Without an "elevator speech," you could miss out on very brief encounters with potential customers for your goods or services. Our daily activities have taken on the speed of our electronic world. You may only get thirty seconds to make an impression. If you botch that opportunity, your bottom line can suffer dire consequences. The precious moment may be lost forever!

The thirty second elevator speech is your verbal, personal introduction to potential customers and referral partners. Without a solid, direct, and informative elevator speech, your word of mouth business referrals are LOST!! Not only should the people listening to you remember your name, but also have a clear idea of how you can help them and other people in their business or industry.

An inappropriate or bungled elevator speech may cause you to lose access to an important sales prospect forever. Picture walking onto an elevator and meeting the perfect candidate for your products or services. You introduce yourself, but then stumble through an obscure description of your offerings. Your ideal client could not figure out what you were trying to say or sell. He gets off the elevator, and you never see him again. How much money and possible referral opportunities have you lost simply by not being prepared? If you botch your elevator speech in a networking setting, not just one prospect, but an entire group of people may not take you or your business seriously. This is why the speech must not only be carefully written, but also thoroughly rehearsed.

The importance of an effective elevator speech became painfully clear in one of my regular networking groups recently. A new gentleman stood up to give his thirty second elevator speech, but other than his name, I was only able to understand the word "computer." After he had given the same rather garbled speech for several weeks, I asked another member of the group about him. He was apparently very skilled at repairing computers and designing Web sites. Needless to say, I was not the only person who did not understand his thirty second introduction. After about two months, he never returned to the group. I hope that he did not think that the group was not supportive, <u>we just could not understand his introduction speech</u>. As a result, we did not take him seriously!!

Remarkably, the elevator speech has been an important part of the business scene for many years. Aileen Pincus described "The Perfect (Elevator) Pitch" in **Bloomberg Business Week** as early as June 18, 2007:

"One of the most important things a business person can do—especially an owner or someone who is involved in sales—is learn how to speak about their business to others. Being able to sum up unique aspects of your service or product in a way that excites others should be a fundamental skill. Yet many executives pay little attention to the continuing development of 'the elevator pitch'—the quick, succinct summation of what your company makes or does.

That's too bad, because the elevator pitch—so named because it should last no longer than the average elevator ride—is far too important to take casually. It's one of the most effective methods available to reach new buyers and clients with a winning message. True, you may not actually be doing the pitching in an elevator, but even if your meeting is a planned, sit-down event, you should still be prepared to capture your audience's attention quickly."

Ms. Pincus went on to admonish the business speaker to "keep it fresh." Constantly update your elevator speech to reflect changing times and values. She continued by advising that the pitch must operate under the motto, "Be Prepared."

Vivian Giang also wrote some helpful ideas about the elevator speech in her article, "How To Sell Yourself In 30 Seconds And Leave People Wanting More" which appeared online in **Business Insider** on November 14, 2003.

She said: "<u>Know exactly where you want to go</u>. Your elevator pitch should answer three questions: Who are you? What do you do? Where do you want to go, or what are you looking for? You need to know exactly what you want to achieve or no one can help you get there."

Ms. Giang also said "<u>Eliminate jargon</u>. You need to be able to explain what you do and who you are in a way that appeals to most people. This means avoiding acronyms or terminology that wouldn't be understood by someone outside of your industry."

She continued by saying, "<u>Pitch it (your speech) to your friends and colleagues</u>. After you've got your story down, practice your elevator pitch with friends and colleagues. Ask them to give you feedback. Ask them what you should do to make it better. Keep practicing and tweaking your pitch until it's natural for you to say aloud and convincing to the listener."

Here is a step by step method of creating your elevator introduction. You will need to update this short speech from time to time in order for it to be effective and to focus on different offering of goods or services. Use the steps and explanations below to help you design your own "perfect pitch."

1. Clearly identify the challenges and problems that your business can solve.

2. Find out all you can about your audience.

3. Write, practice, and time the speech. Secure honest feedback.

4. Revise as necessary for different groups and situations.

1. Clearly identify the challenges and problems that your business can solve.

Businesses sell goods and services. Clarify what you are selling; then, identify how these goods and/or services will positively impact the customer.

Example: If your business sells long lasting, but energy efficient light bulbs for factory use, you might point out that factory employees suffer less fatigue and are more productive when they work in a space which uses your light bulbs.

Use the spaces below to identify the business problems that your products or services solve.

Business problem
Product or service solution

_____

_____

1. Find out all you can about your audience

A. What difficulties can you help them avoid or solve by using your products or services?

_____

B. Who is your typical/best customer?

_____

C. Where can you find and contact your best customer?

_____

D. What special needs does your best customer have?

_____

E. How can you address these special needs?

_____

2. Write, practice, and time the speech. Secure honest feedback.

A. Begin your elevator speech with a question or problem with which all of your potential customers will resonate.

B. Then make a statement about how you and your business can help answer this question or solve this problem. Avoid thinking about selling; focus on how you can help solve problems through your business solutions.

C. Continue by listing ways you can help with this problem or inconvenience.

D. Follow by saying your name and business name.

E. Speak slowly and clearly. Invite the listeners to learn more by speaking with you one on one.

F. Close with a reminder of your name and business name.

**Do not exceed 30 seconds!!

Write a sample elevator speech which includes the products and services that provide solutions for your customers. Use the steps listed A to F above.

A._____

B._____

C._____

D._____

E._____

F._____

**Do not exceed thirty seconds!!!

Secure honest feedback. Practice your speech to make sure that you can perform it without flaws or stumbling over words.

Do not merely "recite" your speech. Make it resonate with your listeners so that they feel compelled to speak with you in person because you can help them solve a problem or reach a goal. Ask your friends to listen to your speech. They can offer valuable feedback if you encourage them to be brutally honest. Practice the way that you will say it when you are face to face with the potential customer. Also practice the way that you will say the speech when you are networking in a large room. These two approaches should be very different both in volume and rate of speech.

Take care to make sure that you can perform the speech in thirty seconds or less. Edward R. Morrow, the most famous news reporter in American history, delivered the news at the average rate of 130 words per minute. This means that your speech cannot contain more than 65 words! Rewrite your speech so that it meets this requirement.

Analyze your speech to see if it feels like a sales pitch rather than a genuine attempt to solve the business or personal problems of the listener. People respond to positively to offers of assistance rather than blatant attempts to manipulate them into purchasing your goods or services. Rewrite your speech so that it focuses on assisting the listener and providing solutions.

3. Revise as necessary for different groups and situations.

Find out everything you can about your potential listeners each time you deliver your speech. The listeners' needs may not match your standard speech. In this case, you will need to be prepared to improvise some part of your presentation to meet the needs of the listeners. Consider what concerns your potential clients might have that are not addressed in your elevator pitch. List them below:

Consider how you can integrate these new concerns into your standard elevator pitch. Practice so that you can be prepared to include or substitute these additional concerns into your speech without exceeding your thirty second time limit.

Another alternative is to have **several versions** of your standard elevator speech. With several elevator speeches that have been carefully crafted and rehearsed, you can be ready at a moment's notice to make the most of this increasingly important, but compressed opportunity.

Write two or three alternative sentences that can be inserted into your elevator speech according to the occasion and the potential customers who are present.

Version
1: _____

_____

Version
2: _____

_____

Version
3: _____

_____

Remember that you will need to repeat this process as often as your potential customers or products and services change. Do **<u>not</u>** rest on your laurels!!!

The clarity of mission that you identify when writing the elevator speech should inform all of your business decisions. Remember that this speech, however brief, is a key factor in your branding and in all of your business exchanges. Don't make promises that you can't deliver. For example, don't promise overnight delivery unless you are certain that you can make it happen. If you make empty promises, you can easily destroy your business credibility.

Although it is a cliché, the truth is that "you only have one chance to make a first impression." Your elevator speech is that chance!!! Eliminate extra or ineffective words. Rehearse several versions of your elevator speech so that you are prepared for many different opportunities. Also make sure that you can give the speech without faltering or including vocal "ums and ahs." Like an Olympic athlete, your success depends on this brief, but important performance.

If you compare your sales before and after doing serious work on your elevator speech, you will see that your effort and time will create new opportunities and new revenue along with new respect among networking colleagues. Don't miss this chance to begin your journey to doubling your income!

Marie Snider

Marie was born in Ohio and attended private Catholic schools from kindergarten through college. She won a scholarship to Ursuline College for her award-winning acting performance as Helen Keller in *The Miracle Worker*. She completed a double major in English and theatre with a minor in Secondary Education. (That included an overwhelming number of credit hours!!) She completed an M.A.in theatre at Case Western Reserve University. She is fond of saying that a master's degree in theatre and $3.50 will get you a regular cup of coffee almost anywhere.

Marie taught English, speech, and theatre in private schools in Ohio for ten years. Then, she became a property manager. Consider the problem of snow removal for five apartment complexes and three strip shopping centers in Cleveland, Ohio! It is no surprise that she moved to North Carolina to enjoy the Carolina blue sky and Southern charm.

She then taught English and theatre at Orange High School in Hillsborough for many years. After retiring from the world of public school, Marie became the Production Manager at SA Brown Marketing Strategy. She enjoyed the fast-paced world of tradeshow and event planning and is a member of Meeting Planners International. For fun, Marie sings. She is a member of the Durham Savoyards, sings in her church choir, and in the shower. Recently, she joined Earl Hadden's team in The Small Business Success Project. She is "jazzed" about helping small business owners prosper.

Marie is one of four siblings. Her "more mature" mother still teaches water exercise for seniors three days a week. Marie has one brilliant daughter, a fabulous son-in-law, and remarkable granddaughter. Besides singing, she loves to travel, read, and dine out with friends.

Contact Marie at marie@smallbizsuccessproject.com

919.451.2250

CHAPTER TWELVE

Become a sought after, trusted speaker.
Marie Snider

Create, rehearse, and perform as often as possible, a series of short speeches which offer helpful information to your target audience. A series of helpful and informative speeches will make you the "go to" person for advice and service in your area of expertise and will expand your customer base.

Many networking groups, chambers of commerce, and other business groups are starved for speakers who are well prepared, interesting and offer valuable content. Speaking is a way to get yourself and your products and services in front of more potential clients and customers. The secret to success at speaking engagements is to offer valuable content without giving a sales pitch for the goods and services that you sell. This is a "tightrope" for the potential speaker, but "walking the line" makes you the "go to" expert on your topic and creates other opportunities for you to interact with your potential customer base.

Sharing what you know may seem to be counter intuitive. After all, "knowledge is power." Public speaking establishes you as reputable, knowledgeable, and kind. When you share with others, your gift returns far more than the effort you expended. When you refuse to share your expertise, you can be perceived as insular, stingy, and secretive. Sharing your expertise makes you perceived as generous, helpful, and an expert in your field.

Alexia Vernon's article which appeared in Forbes Magazine on 1/31/2012 lists five ways "to shift your mindset and realize that as an emerging leader with a powerful message, public speaking is actually the easiest way to effectively reach an audience."

She says: **"It's not all about you.** Remind yourself that public speaking is truly an opportunity to share an important message that your audience should hear. When viewing it as an act of service rather than of self-promotion, you keep your focus on those you're speaking to and seeking to help.

Fear is 100-percent normal. It's your body's signal that you are alive, stretching outside your comfort zone and can make a great impact.

Work toward a goal. When developing a presentation, begin with the end in mind: ask yourself, what do I want my audience to do as a result of listening to me?

Mention the evidence. Fill your speech with stories that show how your business has addressed problems and provided solutions for other clients. People yearn for evidence of how others, just like them, have benefited. When you share stories to show rather than tell what is that you do, you simultaneously entertain, inform and build an authentic trust within your audience. The more you demonstrate a keen understanding of a need, the more believable it is that you and what you offer can be the catalyst for their advantage.

Create urgency. Close with a reason to make a decision now. Create offers specific to this audience and that day. If they go home without making a move, they'll probably forget most of what you shared — information, evidence, and all the excitement and interest you evoked! You want people to trust their impulses while firmly grasping 90-100 percent of the case you make, not when they're replaying just a fraction of it."

Christopher Witt, in an article which appeared in *Entrepreneur Magazine* (#72358) in 2004, suggested the following steps to use at a speaking engagement:

"Be focused. Tell people how to do something-one thing.

Slant your subject toward your audience. Keep the basic content the same, but tweak it 10 percent (usually by adapting your examples and stories to your audience). Examples: "Keep it Off-A Program for Professionals Who Travel" (or "for the Confirmed Couch Potato," etc.).

Be brief. Stay within the time limits your host suggests. If possible, speak for 15 to 20 minutes; then take questions from the floor.

Be simple and direct without being simplistic. Tell stories and give examples.

To get your speeches noticed, send press releases to local newspapers, trade journals and business publications."

At first, I worried that my experience as a speech coach and trained public speaker would strike my audience as if I were merely "showing off." However, I noticed a major increase in connections and referrals within my networking groups as soon as I became a regular speaker. I made sure that I shared information that would be helpful to my listeners without really worrying whether it would create an increased client base for me. No one was more surprised than I that more and more people began to seek my help and advice (and eventually hired me to coach them for their own speaking events).

One way to fail miserably and to sabotage a speaking opportunity is to use it as a sales presentation. I watched in horror one time when a member of a group that I was active in used her speaking time as an opportunity to force the audience to sample diet foods that her company supplied. She spent more than half of her allotted time setting up the foods. She then had only a small portion of her presentation to explain why these products were special. She had obviously little regard for the information needs of the group.

She wasted her opportunity to be seen as an expert by turning her presentation into a sales tactic.

One of the worst mistakes that you can make as a speaker is to spend all of your time "pitching" your own products or services. When you speak to a group of business people, **be sure to focus on what they need, not what you want!**

To position yourself as a valuable speaker, consider what needs the group has that you can address. Next, consider what you have to offer that might be useful to the group. Are you an expert at business finance? Planning for business expansion?

Selling a business? Business loans? Creating an effective business calendar? Marketing for small businesses? Social media? Web site design? Business insurance? Business networking? Be sure to choose a topic that will showcase you as an expert.

List the areas of expertise that you might be comfortable presenting:

List three ways that can you leverage these topics in a speech to demonstrate your expertise while providing valuable information for your listeners:

When you plan your speech, consider saving some of your allotted time for questions from the audience. Your listeners will feel more connected to you when you respond to their individual questions in a thoughtful and informative way. Be prepared for these questions by considering in advance what the audience members might ask. Write a list of questions below that you might be asked after you speak on a topic of your expertise.

When The Affordable Care Act was just beginning enrollment, a man who sold insurance for Blue Cross volunteered to speak at one of my networking groups. He was brilliant! In only ten minutes, he explained how the insurance exchanges worked and how those small business owners, whom he called "solopreneurs" might now be able to enjoy the benefits of health insurance. He explained how he worked with his customers to locate affordable Blue Cross insurance plans which still fit within the Federal guidelines. Even those of us who were already happy with our insurance felt that he had eliminated massive confusion about how the Affordable Care Act would work. I know that after his presentation, he was nearly overwhelmed with one on one meetings to talk individually with members of the group. I also know that he exceeded his closing goals for that quarter by a substantial amount which he attributed to this particular speech. He did admit to making the same speech at a number of different networking groups. He was an excellent example of a speaker who offers very helpful content at the right time!

Consider what "hot topics" you can leverage by helping business people understand the pros and cons of various actions. This kind of presentation might be ideal for financial planners, mortgage brokers, and business bankers to use the opportunity to demystify some of the jargon that surrounds their professions. Providing this kind of valuable content creates a short cut in the "know, like, trust" continuum that creates a sale.

List three topics that you can demystify for your listeners:

Imagine what your business will look like when you have completed a series of helpful speeches in which you give the audience valuable content which is useful whether or not they engage you! These speaking engagements may not always result in immediate sales to the listeners, but they will make your name the first one that your listeners think of when they are asked if anyone knows someone who can help them with the problem or difficulty that you detailed in your speech. You will quickly go from one of the people who sells particular goods or services to the expert to talk to in this situation! Speaking makes you the "go to" person in regards to your area of expertise.

Now for the elephant in the room!!! Fear of public speaking is very common!!! Being anxious about giving a presentation is normal, even for experienced speakers. Preparation is the key to feeling more relaxed. NEVER speak "off the cuff" to a large group of listeners. Your speech, no matter how long or short, must be carefully crafted and rehearsed. You must practice your speech and memorize your main points in advance. You must anticipate questions and be prepared to answer them. Enlist the help of friends and colleagues for practice sessions. In addition, if you are serious about speaking, Toastmasters International is a good resource for helping business people get experience and become more competent as public speakers.

Don't miss out on an excellent way to build your business and become a recognized expert in your field. Start to today to become a sought after speaker!

See Chapter 11 for Marie Snider's biography.

CHAPTER THIRTEEN

Build your credibility and authority.
Diana M. Needham

Build your authority to explode your income and value to your market.

Leverage your knowledge and experience to gain leadership status in your market.

When you are viewed as an authority, you'll be the one chosen over your competitors and can demand higher fees. You'll no longer chase leads and prospects; instead they find you and your offerings.

We are living in one of the most exciting times for entrepreneurs, authors, speakers, and consultants to take advantage of the almost limitless opportunities to access strategies used by national business gurus, to establish instant credibility and trust. So why are so many business owners, speakers, coaches, and consultants struggling to gain attention while others, perhaps even *less qualified or deserving*, are being recognized as the expert ... the AUTHORITY in their industry?

It's not necessarily because they are better or smarter at their craft. In fact, that's rarely the case. The truth is, they are doing the right things that make it easy *for others to call them the expert*. More importantly, *they are not waiting* for someone else to come and "anoint" them as the authority. They are *taking control and architecting their ascent* with *clear purpose and a plan*.

There are many more ways to do it *wrong* (in strategy application) than there are to do it right. Most business owners are doing it wrong or completely neglecting it all together. Before you ever make a decision on a website, a video, social media, book, or any kind of content for that matter, you need to know how you are going to apply these strategies to your business to get the most effective authority positioning.

The Importance of your message.

You need to understand what your message is, who your message is for, and why your message will inspire authority, regardless of which medium you use to deliver it. Ask yourself now "Who do I help and how do I help them?" *Link to marketing chapter?*

A successful message will position you as an authority, inspiring prospects to choose you, and makes your current clients want to come back more often to spend more money, and tell their friends, family and even strangers about how great you are.

If your message is off-target, it doesn't really matter how many websites, videos or books in which you have invested time, money, and effort. Your results will fall short and be less than stellar.

Take the time to understand how to get prospects to "choose you" over your competitors, how to turn prospects into clients, and then turn those clients into fans by positioning yourself as the authority in your industry. Like a skilled architect, create *your authority with a purposely designed plan*.

What is authority marketing?

Authority Marketing is the process of positioning yourself as an authority in your market using different forms of media. Times are changing and to attract attention to your brand, you need to not only promote your business, but also to promote *yourself* as a brand.

Marketing Expert, Dan Kennedy says "The simple truth is, if you aren't deliberate, systematically, methodically or rapidly and dramatically establishing yourself as a celebrity, at least to your clientele and target market, you are asleep at the wheel, ignoring what is fueling the entire economy around you, neglecting development of a measurably valuable asset."

In the book *The Art of War*, the famous general Sun Tzu said "When you are small, you need to appear big." While he likely did not mean for this simple statement to apply to marketing advice, it is indeed an incredibly important point to remember when positioning yourself as an authority in your industry. Size is not the issue. Strategy is.

To some, becoming an authority is synonymous with being the expert or thought leader. Many think expert or authority status can only be attained by convincing enough people that they are smarter than everyone else in their field. Neither of these is correct.

What authority positioning is not.

Here are the 5 myths that so many entrepreneurs believe regarding what it takes to be a recognized authority.

Myth #1. To be an expert, I just need to call myself the expert.

This has been a popular theory for many years. While this may have been somewhat effective in the past, it is not how we see most industry leaders achieve their success and reach real authority status.

It goes far beyond that. We can no longer simply call ourselves an expert and expect the masses to take us at our word. However you can easily be the person that takes the actions that will make it ***easy for others***   to call **you** the expert.

That is what real authority is: *having others recognize you as the expert, and it is simpler than most make it out to be.*

Myth #2. An expert is a person that knows everything about their industry and subject matter.

The truth is, such a person does not exist. No one knows everything there is about his or her industry, and those that claim they do actually diminish their credibility because people know it is not possible.

An expert is someone that knows enough to be able to do 2 things: 1. help their customers and their prospects, and 2) be willing to share that knowledge.

Myth #3. *An expert is the very best at what they do in their field.*

Think of someone right now who is considered an expert or an authority in your industry, whether it's fitness, marketing, financial, personal development, coaching, or real estate. Go ahead and picture that person in your mind. Now ask yourself, "Does this person really know any more than I do? Are they the best at what they do?"

So why are they considered the authority? More importantly, *why aren't you?*

Myth # 4. *It takes years to build an expert reputation so that credible media will recognize you as an authority.*

That is the slow road that most people take, if they take the road to authority status at all. This is just an excuse, a logical explanation or justification that we can 'lean on' as to why we have not yet achieved expert status.

Most people think that to be considered an expert, they have to work years to build up their reputation by gaining more knowledge, and doing that one more thing that will allow them to convince others that they are an expert at what they do. Then maybe, just maybe, someone, some day, people will come along and recognize us as an expert. Then even the media will start to talk about us.

It's a nice story we tell ourselves. It helps us feel that expert and authority status is coming. It's just down the road. "Down the road"… that is a dangerous thing to wait for, especially since the reality is that you can position yourself in the media as an expert *right now*. You can let others see you as an authority because third party credible sources are already talking about you *as* that expert.

Myth #5. I'm not ready to step up as an authority right now.

One of the big obstacles many hard working entrepreneurs place in front of themselves is questioning their own authority.

"Am I really an authority? Am I really an expert? I don't know everything about everything in my industry. I'm just not comfortable calling myself an expert yet … but definitely down the road."

Write this down, burn it into your brain:

It is not about calling yourself an expert!

Let's get this out of the way right now. Commit to yourself that you will never call *yourself* an expert again. Commit to yourself that you **will** freely allow **others** to call you the expert. Starting right now.

Answer these questions. Don't hesitate or do them later. Do not read another word until you answer these two simple questions.

(1) Do you generally know more than your prospects about your industry, your product, or your service?

(2) Are you willing and able to help your prospects?

If you answered yes to these two questions, then to me and many of your prospects, you are an EXPERT.

What makes you an expert?

Here is the simple truth: You know more than your prospects and clients, and you are willing and able to help them.

Think that's too simple? Let's examine some of the most popular business celebrities from different industries and figure out why they are perceived to be authorities in their field.

Look at people like Dave Ramsey, Suze Orman, Doctor Oz, or Gary Vaynerchuk, and think about their authority positioning in their particular field.

- Are they the smartest in their fields?
- Are they the best at what they do in their field?
- , Do they know everything about everything in their industry?

And now that you are thinking about it, do they actually ever call themselves an expert? Do they refer to themselves as THE Authority?

How often do you see them yelling: "Buy my stuff! Buy my stuff!"? Rarely, if ever, right?

What really constitutes an "authority?"

So why are they perceived as authorities, even though they are not doing any of the things that so many would have you believe you need to do to be considered the expert?

They are not the smartest, and they are not the best. They do not call themselves the expert, and they are not constantly shouting for you to buy their stuff.

Why? Perhaps it's because they happen to know more than their prospects and customers, and they are willing and able to help them.

So ask yourself again: If Suze Orman, Doctor Oz, or Dave Ramsey are not the best, if they are not the smartest and if they do not know everything about everything about their field, then why are they the authorities? Why are they the expert celebrities in their fields?

There really is a simple answer.

It is because they are ***educators and advocates for the success of their prospects and customers***.

Read that once more. It is probably the most important point in this chapter and the reason that you will be recognized as an authority sooner rather than later.

Starting today, purposely remove any fears, worries or pressure that you may have put on yourself to call yourself an expert or to convince others that you're the expert. Simply replace "I'm an expert" with "I'm an educator and an advocate for the success of my customers and my prospects."

Do that once or twice a day and you will see something remarkable begin happen. You will immediately find yourself in the same position as the celebrity authorities in your field!

When you put yourself in the frame of mind of being the educator and the advocate for the success of your prospects and customers, then you will find that you never have to call *yourself* an expert again.

Others will call you the expert.

Here are some other unfair realities when it comes to authority:

When it comes to attracting new customers ...

- It really does not matter if you have a college degree.
- It does not matter how many products you have purchased.
- It does not matter how many events you have attended.
- It does not even matter how hard you work or how good you really are.

Building Trust is paramount.

A recent study conducted by an international market research organization (AP-GfK), suggests only one third of Americans say that 'most people can be trusted.' If your prospects do not trust or believe you, if they are not convinced that you are an authority, you will have to work ten times as hard to convert them into a customer.

If, however, your prospects **do** trust that you are an authority; if they see others looking at you as an authority; if they see you being an educator and an advocate for their success; then they will choose you over your competition, **even if it costs them more to work with you.**

Perception is reality. Like it or not, our society has been conditioned to see the media as a credible source of information. We trust the media. We are influenced by media recommendations. We give authority to those that are endorsed and seen in the media.

Reader's Digest recently said that the four most trusted people in the world were Tom Hanks, Sandra Bullock, Denzel Washington and Meryl Streep. The truth is, they are no smarter than you are; no better than you are. In fact, you are probably brilliant compared to ninety-nine percent of the so-called experts featured in the media.

So here is the simple formula. **Get media sources and third party people talking about you as an educator and advocate can create instant authority for you and your business**.

How does Authority Marketing help you?

You may be asking, "Just how does authority marketing help me?" It is all about positioning yourself so you stand apart from your competitors, and are known as THE leading authority and expert in your industry. You become the one sought out rather than the one chasing prospects. You'll no longer chase leads and prospects; instead they find you and your offerings.

Authority marketing offers several benefits to you and your business.

Build credibility and trust

When someone sees you consistently quoted in the media, it builds that perception of added trust and credibility. It even positions you to gain more media coverage. Journalists scour LinkedIn for interviewees and determine that anyone who is acclimated to media coverage is normally labeled as a safe bet for additional interviews.

Increase conversions

You can leverage the traffic you are already receiving by having higher conversions, and conversions mean sales. When someone is searching for you by name, they are further down the sales funnel and they are ready to hire someone. You are competing for attention. It is usually down to you and one competitor. By being featured and quoted in the media, you stand out from your competitors, thus making the choice easier for a customer to choose you.

Become an educator and advocate for your customers

If you concentrate on being an educator and advocate for the success of your customers and position yourself this way, it eliminates the buyer/seller positioning. You'll also be known as the "go-to-person" in your industry.

Become a consistent contributor in the media

When you continually offer helpful information that is easy to apply, people will start to trust you and respect your knowledge and expertise. Focus on one problem at a time and keep it simple. This is how you start to build your authority in your market.

Become a business celebrity

This is a great part of the authority marketing process. When you engage in business spotlight articles that are syndicated in national media outlets, you can add media names or logos to all your marketing materials (website, social profiles, business cards, brochures, signage, etc.). You won't have to call yourself an expert … everyone else will do that for you.

You've no doubt noticed profile images that include media logos are now showing up on social media. Some consider using media a key component in building their authority positioning. Ask yourself if this kind of branding would elevate you in the eyes of your ideal prospects and clients.

Other ways to build your authority.

Becoming trustworthy and credible online is an important part of the journey. Here are some online and offline activities that can build your authority with your market.

- Write a book that positions you as a leader and authority in your field.
- Hone your public speaking skills and speak often on your area of focus.
- Build your online social media presence, especially on LinkedIn link to LN chapter.

How do I get started?

First, answer these 2 questions.

1. Do you know more than your prospects about your industry, your product, or your service?
2. Are you willing and able to help your prospects?

The answer is Yes to both questions, right? Then the next key step is to *decide* to claim your authority. No more waiting for someone else to recognize or "anoint" you.

Using the chart below, assess honestly where you are now and what are the top few next steps.

- Which of these authority "assets" do you currently have?
- What do you need to focus on as the next step to building your authority, both online and offline?

Asset	Have or Not	Comments/Next Steps
Strong, well-defined personal brand		
Professionally shot photos		
Professionally done logo		
Well-defined 60 second introduction to use at networking events		
Client-attracting personal story		
Consistent image on social media		
Wardrobe fits the professional image I want to portray		
I have been featured as an authority in major affiliate news (NBC, Fox, CBS, ABC)		
I have my own published content		
✓ My own book		
✓ CD's		
✓ DVD's		
✓ Podcast		
✓ Videos		
I have a professionally done promotion brochure or flyer		
I have professionally written copy to attract clients		
I speak publicly frequently to grow my business and expand my authority position		

See Chapter 9 for Diana Needham's biography.

CHAPTER FOURTEEN

Create momentum with your promotional products.
Randy Bernstein

Choose promotional giveaways so that they create an impetus to purchase your goods or services. The giveaway should reflect your business and appeal to your target audience. In addition, it should be used by your target audience whenever he or she is likely to make the decision to purchase your goods or services.

With the correct selection of a branded promotional item, given out in a meaningful way, you will continue to remind people of your business long after your trade show is over.

You are spending somewhere between $200 and $2000 (or more) for a vendor booth at a trade show. You have been sending out email messages to your potential clients asking them to attend. You have eye-catching displays and beautiful brochures ready to hand out, and you've lined up staff to work the booth. At the last minute, you decide that you want some give-a-ways for the booth.

You call your local promotional person and say, "I have a trade show coming up, and I need some cheap pens to give away."

You are making quite an investment of money and time in your booth. This give-a-way is something that the potential customers will take with them to remember you. If you give them a "cheap pen," what is that saying about your business?

Your give-a-way should be economical, value conscious, within budget. Yes, yes, and yes! But cheap---definitely NO!!

Don't even get me started on pens as trade show give-a-ways. Take a look in your desk drawer or the cup on your desk. How many pens with logos do you have? Most likely, your "cheap pen" is going to get stuck in the drawer or cup, never to be seen again until your "lost customer" moves to a new desk or new office and tosses away all of the cheap pens with the rest of the junk!

You are probably asking yourself, "What should I give away?" To determine the answer, consider your ideal customer and your business. Also consider the brand image that you want to convey. Then, decide how many promotional items you will need and what your budget is for these give-a-ways.

The most important objective with any branded promotional item is that it is something that the recipient wants. Consider when they will want it, where they will keep it, and how they will use it. When they do use the item, they will see your company name and remember you when they need your product or service!

To make this happen, first you must consider your ideal customer who will attend this trade show. This may be only one group in your target market, but this must be the group that you will encounter at the event. Depending on the trade show, these potential customers could be homeowners, parents, business executives, brides-to-be, pet owners or some other group.

Once you have identified your target group for this particular trade show, think about the help that they need. I don't mean how your business can help them. Save that for your great presentation and fancy brochure. Consider the help that you will provide for them via a branded promotional product that they will want, keep, and use. You want them remember you and your business each time they use your valued promotional item!

For example:

Homeowners need items that make their life easier such as jar openers, refrigerator magnets, or magnetic dry erase boards for grocery lists.

Business executives need things for their desk such as notepads, sticky notes, letter openers, and paper clip dispensers.

Brides can use sewing kits, first aid kits, hand fans, and tissue packets.

Pet owners need waste bags, flashing lights for a dog collar for nighttime walks, and travel water bowls.

Not only will these items be needed by the recipient, they will be used in the place where the potential customer is going to make a decision about using your products or services. These kinds of promotional items go a long way toward making the recipients remember YOU and your business!

Now that you've identified your target market for the trade show and the kinds of promotional items that would appeal to them, you need to make sure that those items reflect your business. For example, if you are a technology company, notepads and pens are contrary to your business. Instead, consider cell phone holders, charging adapters, and other tech products.

Most promotional products will work for a variety of businesses. It's a good idea to do a check to make sure that the item you choose is a good fit for your business.

Before we talk about how many items you will need and your budget, let's talk about the event where you will be giving these items out. Picture this. It's the day of the show-the booth is decorated, the brochures are laid out. Your booth staff is sharply dressed, branded, and ready to talk about your business. The only thing left is to put a bunch of your promotional items on the table for people to grab, right? WRONG!!!

Your carefully selected and branded promotional items should not be freebies, but earned when a potential customer stops to learn about your business.

When somebody grabs your promotional items off the table, it means nothing to them except something they got for free. If you are a wedding photographer, that bride-to-be who grabbed your $3 sewing kit might already have a wedding photographer lined up. You just wasted $3! That's not a lot, but it will add up over the course of the event.

Instead, keep your promotional items behind the counter. When someone stops to speak with you, reach behind the counter when you are wrapping up your conversation and pick up one of your useful promotional items branded with your business name and contact information. Give to your booth guest while explaining that it is a gift in appreciation for their time. Not a doodad, trinket, "whatchamacallit," or bauble, but a GIFT!!

It may not seem like much to you, but to the recipient, you are probably the only person at the event who gave them a gift. They were expecting only a sales pitch, but you gave them a gift. They will appreciate that gesture, and they will feel good about your company. They will say, "Thank you!" to you. How many times do you have people stop to hear your sales pitch and then thank you?

When they get home after the trade show, they will look through the items that they "picked up." All but one of them will have no meaning because they were just greedily grabbed off of the tables. Only your item was given as a gift. They will remember the gift and your conversation whenever they use the promotional item.

Now that you grasp how you will use your branded promotional items, you can better estimate how many you will need.

Estimate how many people you expect to stop by your booth to learn about your company and increase this number by 25% to be sure that you don't run out. This is the number of promotional items that you will need for the event. This is a much smaller number than you would need if you just put them on the table for people to grab.

Consider your budget for promotional items for this event. I am not asking what you are willing to pay per item, but your overall budget for the event. You had a budget for the booth, for the booth staff, and meals throughout the day. You should also have a budget for promotional items.

Since the promotional items are going to be used as a gift to people who stop to learn more about your company, you will distribute fewer items. That means that you will be able to spend more on each gifted promotional item. While the staff in other booths are giving out or permitting people to grab cheap pens, you will give out carefully considered valuable, useful and carefully branded items as GIFTS.

Long after the display booths are boxed up, the sales people are home with their families, and the potential clients have recycled their brochures, the branded promotional items that you gave as gifts will continue to be used by potential future clients. As they use these items, they will see your company name and contact information over and over. When they need your product or service, they will know who to call. That's when that branded promotional item becomes a gift to you!

My client, Jerry Dillard, of Jerry Dillard Photography, sent me a note of thanks for his success using my approach to promotional giveaways:

"I would like to thank Randy Bernstein for his help in my wedding venue events. I wanted to have a handout for brides that would be more than just a pen or sticky notes. Randy showed me a small sewing kit. This was a great way to start conversations with brides by having them guess what the item was. A great icebreaker! It has, over the years, proved to be a great investment and has lead to many weddings and referrals. I know that this investment paid for itself many times over."

Randy Bernstein

Randy Bernstein is the owner of BrandShark, a promotional product company helping businesses across the United States make memorable impressions.

For 25+ years, Randy was in the corporate world, helping some of the largest banks in the country find optimal solutions for their development projects. It is this "client focused solution" mentality that he brings to the promotional product industry.

Since 2008, Randy has been working with businesses to help them increase their visibility by finding the right promotional items for their business focus, target market, and their budget. Randy takes pride in the fact that he does not sell products, but offers solutions to business needs. He only feels successful when the people with whom he is working feel successful.

Randy is also an ambassador for the Durham Chamber of Commerce, serves on an advisory board for the Durham Tech Community College Small Business Center, holds a leadership role in the Bull City Business Leaders chapter of Business Networking International, and is a District Committee Member for the Shakori District of the Boy Scouts of America.

Originally from Chicago, Randy and his wife Donna Dillehay, a Durham, NC native and President of Self and Associates, CPAs, now reside in Hillsborough, NC. They have two sons, Justin and Aaron. They celebrated their 28th wedding anniversary last June.

Contact - Randy@TheBrandShark.com
LinkedIn - www.linkedin.com/in/RandyBernstein
Website - www.TheBrandShark.com

Online Marketing
and Social Media

CHAPTER FIFTEEN

Provide access to your content anywhere, and on any device by leveraging the power of video to show off your products and services.
Pete C. Goswick

Instead of writing pages of text, video gives you the power to "visually show off" your product or service and explain the benefits in half the time. People stick around and learn more about you and/or your company.

If a picture worth a 1,000 words then a 5 minute video is worth 8,970 words... (There are 29.9 pictures per second of video.) Video engages the viewer much more that written text. It is one thing to write down the reasons why someone should buy your product/service. But, it is quite another to actually see your product/service in action. Using video is your opportunity to truly show off everything your product or service can do.

Today people are hungry for information but want it fast. So they'd prefer to spend 2-3 minutes watching a video rather than spending 15-20 minutes reading text. Moreover, videos also help businesses to communicate their important points to their target audience in very little time.

Creating videos can help keep people engaged with your products/services, especially if you add in a little humor. With video you can show off the top features of your products/services while also sharing your brand personality. It's always best to give people the information they need as quickly as you can while also keeping it interesting...video is the perfect way to do that.

Instead of writing pages of text, videos give you the power to "visually show off" your product or service and explain the benefits in half the time. People stick around and learn more about you and/or your company. The more engaging your video, the more opportunity you have to pull them into your marketing environment and hopefully encourage them to make a purchase in the future.

With the power of Google and the invention of YouTube, people expect to be able to access any content, anywhere, and on any device. So, make sure your video is available to them no matter where they are. Create a company YouTube channel and post quick informational videos. Add videos to your website. Create video ads. Having videos on multiple platforms will help ensure that you can reach people anywhere.

A study by A.C. Nielsen in 2011 reported that approximately 76% of US citizens spend 43 hours a month on the Internet. During this time they viewed more than 3,237 web pages, including videos. In 2012, people in the US watched more than 21 billion videos online, which indicates that video marketing can be the most powerful way to reach to target markets.

One of the biggest advantages of video marketing is that is helps you to reach out to millions of people within a short time, without spending too many of your marketing dollars. There is no other form of marketing that can offer such impressive results at such a reasonable price.

One of the best advantages of video marketing is that it increases the duration that a person spends on a web page. Your target audience will remember what they saw and heard. Video is one of the best ways to present your products/service and to explain how they work. Today, you can use social media and emails to distribute your videos as well.

An advantage of video marketing is that videos you create will last for years and will get you more exposure with time. Usually ads die out within a short time, but the opposite is true with videos. You can continue to reap benefits with video for years.

Your audience craves visual content. Our brains love images. Did you know we process visuals 60,000 times faster than text? That's an important fact to keep in mind as you develop your social media marketing plans. If you have an important message you need to get out or just want to stand out from the crowd, video is the way to go.

Here are just a few examples that demonstrate people are watching online videos:

- **YouTube** is the world's 3rd most-visited website! Recently, it has surpassed Facebook. In fact, it is now the 2nd most-visited website.
- **YouTube** is considered the number two search engine right behind Google (People want video answers).
- **YouTube** is now more popular than cable television.
- **YouTube** now receives over 5 billion daily views… and that number is rapidly growing.
- **YouTube** mobile gets over 1 billion views per day!

Why YouTube for my video hosting platform? YouTube is not just about videos of cute babies and kitty cats anymore. Large companies such as Ford Motor Company, Apple, BestBuy, Coca-Cola and many others all have a significant presence on YouTube. YouTube is the largest and most visited video hosting site in the world. It doesn't cost an outrageous amount of money to have a very effective and professional presence on YouTube. Your business can be on the same level as the "big boys" for **free.** One of the biggest benefits to using YouTube is that Google owns YouTube and rewards people that use YouTube with better results in Google search results.

Google, Yahoo, Bing, and other search engines rank websites featuring video content highly. Many big brands tend to embed YouTube videos into their homepages and other primary pages. You can upload videos to your YouTube channel; and then, embed them in your web pages. Search engines will love you for it!

YouTube videos are some of the most shared types of content on the Web. A video with only 10,000 viewers can bring your business huge exposure. When that video promotes a product or service, it always means increased sales. The conclusion is that YouTube marketing has many advantages that simply cannot be ignored.

People look for helpful videos that solve their problems and give them practical tips. They form a favorable opinion of those who create them. By showcasing your expertise through YouTube videos, you gain the trust of customers. In turn, those customers will be more likely to buy your products or services. Not every business has the time or energy to create and distribute free content that helps customers though, but those that do stand out.

Marketing with YouTube is a highly effective way of building trust. By creating insider videos, you give faces to the people who run your business. If the faces are honest and friendly, you will be liked. It is extremely important for people to feel like they "know, like and trust" you or your business. Video can help!

A few tips on creating a marketing video.

1. Make your title count. There are two main reasons why the title is so important. One, a great title can instantly grabs a viewer's attention. Two, when you use the appropriate keywords in your title you are more likely to show up on search engines when people are searching for your topic. As mentioned before, Google owns YouTube, so there's a connection between video and searching.

2. Provide excellent content. Take some time to think about your ideal viewer. "How-to" videos are extremely successful because not only do they offer great value to your viewer, but also you're able to showcase your knowledge and skill, therefore positioning yourself as an expert.

3. No matter how good your content is, it won't matter if your video is too long and you lose your viewer's attention. Try to keep it short.

4. Have your company logo displayed prominently somewhere on the screen.

5. Always provide an HTML link. When you post on YouTube you have the option to write a short description of your video. Always start with the link you want to drive your viewers to, so you don't miss this key opportunity.

6. Go beyond YouTube. Be sure to always embed your video on your own website. This will increase the amount of time people spend on your website and help grow a captive audience. Also, Google's algorithms consider how many times a video is viewed, and embedded video views you receive get added to the 'views' tally on YouTube. This is important for showing up in Google search results!

7. Always Include a Call to Action. Never miss the opportunity to ask your viewers to take some type of action at the end of your video. You can ask them to sign up for your newsletter, go to a specific website, leave a comment about your video or visit your blog. If your video is good you'll likely have their full attention. Make sure to take advantage of it.

8. Optimize your video so it will be found by the search engines when someone enters the keyword(s) you want to rank for. This is especially important for local searches.

9. Watch other marketing videos to see what "best practices" can be learned from them. If you are a plumber, do a YouTube search for plumber and see how other plumbers are using YouTube in their marketing efforts. Learn from like-minded people.

10. Remember, "**Bad audio means bad video**." I truly believe that audio makes up 80% (or more) of the viewing experience. If your audio sounds like you are in a barrel or too low or too loud people will leave without watching your video...no matter how good the image is. Take the time to insure the audio quality matches (or even exceeds) the video quality.

Four easy go-to types of videos you might make:
1. Personal, talking heads videos.
2. Customer testimonial videos – very effective.
3. Product demonstration videos – people want to see "how to" videos.
4. Screen capture videos – you don't even have to be on-screen.

Just like any other marketing campaign, video marketing requires thought and planning. Here are just a few things to keep in mind when considering whether or not to use video to market your products/services:

- The chances of getting a page 1 listing on Google are 53 times greater using video.
- A website visitor will stay 2 minutes longer when you have a video on your site.
- By 2017 video will be 90% of all Internet traffic.
- 65% of people visit the website after watching the video.
- Over 1 billion unique visitors frequent YouTube monthly.

- 87% of social media users follow their brand's videos
- Posts with video attract 3 times more visitors.

Here is an example of how video can make a difference. I had a client that did not have any presence on the first couple of pages of Google. I created a video using a review that they had received from one of their customers. It was a very professional looking video that spoke about my client and the good service the customer had received. Within days of posting the video to You Tube, they were listed on the first page of Google (the only video on the first page). My client was extremely pleased and has contracted with me to do more review videos for him.

Don't miss out on the value of video!! I hope to watch some great videos about you and your products/services on YouTube very soon.

Pete C. Goswick

Pete has an extensive background in information technology. He started in the field as a computer operator in 1969 and rose to position of Director, Alumni & Development Systems at Duke University. In 2001 Pete left Duke and began his journey as an entrepreneur by forming Viewpoint Video Services. In the beginning Pete and his wife, Jenny Barwick, had pleasure of working with many folks as they honed their skills a videographers. In the beginning they primarily videoed weddings, dance recitals, funerals, public speakers, etc. As Pete became more skilled he branched out and began offering video services to the legal community. He primarily videoed legal depositions for attorneys and sometimes was used for court room presentation support.

In 2013 Pete got involved in internet marketing, specifically video marketing and online reputation marketing for local small/medium businesses. With his extensive background in information technology this was a perfect fit for him. Pete has a passion for trying to help local small/medium businesses compete with other large businesses and believes the internet helps level the playing field.

Pete grew up in North Carolina and has a deep appreciation for the small local business person and he firmly believes they are the lifeblood of the local economy. "Buy Local" is something that he tries to do whenever possible.

Between Jenny and Pete they have five adult children, four great daughters-in-law and four beautiful grandchildren. They also have two cats and a "yeller dog." Pete enjoys college sports especially basketball. He is a former baseball umpire and basketball referee. He also really like keeping up with all his old high school friends on Facebook.

For more information and to connect with Pete you can find him at:

- ncVideographer@gmail.com
- www.linkedin.com/in/viewpointvideo
- www.youtube.com/user/viewpointvideo
- twitter.com/ViewpointPete
- www.facebook.com/ViewpointVideoMarketing

plus.google.com/+ViewpointVideoandWebMarketingDurham/

CHAPTER SIXTEEN

**Build your 5-star reputation online and market that reputation
to get more customers.
Pete C. Goswick**

"There is no advertisement as powerful as a positive reputation traveling fast" – Brian Koslow

Everyday people go online searching for products or services. One of the most important things they look for is the reputation of the business offering the products or services. They want to know what experience other people had in purchasing the product or service. No one wants a bad experience. What others are saying carries a lot of weight in the buying decision. If three services were virtually identical except Service A had 4 good reviews and 2 bad reviews, Service B had no reviews at all, and Service C had 6 five-Star reviews the likelihood is that Service C would get more calls. The online marketing game has changed. The businesses with the 5-Star online reputation have the advantage.

What people say about your company online has become the single most important reflection of your company's quality, reliability, and skill. It doesn't matter if you're a dentist, a plastic surgeon, a carpet cleaner, or a painter…

72% If buyers trust reviews as much as personal recommendations. Source: BrightLocal

70% Trust consumer reviews posted on line. Source: Nielsen

70% Of consumers trust a business with minimum of 6- 10 reviews. Sources: Demandforce, Economist.com, Searchengineland.com, BrightLocal

Reputation marketing is the process of building a 5-Star reputation online, and then marketing that reputation to get more customers. It is more than reputation management. Management implies maintenance…it's passive. Marketing is active, and it's the point at which your business makes more money. Reputation marketing includes reputation management.

There are four basic types of reputation based on reviews: bad reputation, no reputation, good reputation, and a 5-Star reputation. Neither of the first two will get your phone ringing. Good reviews are likely to have a mix of good and not-so-good reviews. However, even this can hurt you, especially if the just "OK" reviews are at the top. If your competitor has slightly better reviews, it is likely he/she will "eat your lunch." You need to have at least ten 5-Star reviews online to ensure that customers call you.

Your number one marketing priority should be developing a 5-Star online reputation. All of your other marketing efforts, whether they be online such as SEO, social media, PPC, or offline such as direct mail, magazines, radio, or TV, will ultimately lead the consumer to learn more about you online. There, "your less than stellar" or "non-existent" reputation drives them away. Most business owners fail to realize is that what consumers want is information that will help them feel confident they're making the best purchase. Today, quite a bit of that confidence comes in the form of online reviews reflecting others' experiences.

Reputation Marketing means your most satisfied customers do the selling for you. Imagine the powerful influence that 5-Star reviews from hundreds of your satisfied customers will have on showing potential customers that you are the best choice and the market leader. That's what a 5-Star online reputation can do for your business.

Marketing that 5-Star reputation is the greatest opportunity there has ever been to seize an advantage over your competition and establish yourself as the clear choice and market leader among consumers where you do business. To do nothing means to invite your competition to take that lead while you just watch it happen online.

Reputation Management vs. Reputation Marketing

The goal of online reputation management services is to bury the bad online content and highlight the good. In most cases, the reputation management service will have to produce a lot of search engine optimized content to bury the bad and link to the good. In the end, the goal is to have the first few pages of the search engines coming up with positive content about your business.

The difference is reputation marketing is more proactive than reactive. Also, there are only a hand full of companies that can do this properly with dedicated systems in place that find all bad reviews and information rather than just specific key words that you type in. Most companies rely on scraping tools which are inaccurate in most cases.

Online reputation management services *after* you market the 5-Star reputation first are extremely important and are only going to grow in importance as people become more connected. So whether you're a clothing company that has been getting a lot of bad online talk about the conditions under which your clothing is produced or your company has been involved in scandals in the past, you should be marketing your 5-Star reputation first, and then managing your overall reputation secondly and carefully.

So how do you actually do reputation marketing?

First, you need to build your reputation. This involves finding your reviews online, claiming your public listings like Google, Yelp, Bing and repairing bad reviews if possible.

Next, employ sales strategies to leverage your great reputation online.

After that, you need to manage your reputation which includes monitoring it.

Step four is to create a culture in your business that invites 5-Star reviews and reduces the chance of a negative review. Anyone in your business can have an off-day when it comes to serving a customer, but you want to keep these to a minimum and repair the damage as quickly as possible. The fact is that you are always only one review away from a bad reputation. If this sounds tiring and discouraging, it doesn't have to be once your culture is established.

Some say that your reputation is all you have. Once it is tarnished, it is very hard to recover. If you think about your own judgment process about selecting a place to do business, your impression of the reputation of the business will absolutely impact your decision to buy. Now, there are exceptions: a gas station with a lousy reputation 60 miles from the next station when your gauge is on empty; a grungy convenience store that has cold water when you really need it; an airline you hate that has the last flight home or you spend the night in No Where, USA. Those are exceptions. But, by and large, when you have a poor impression about a business, you look elsewhere. That is why businesses, more and more, are very conscious of their reputations. They go great lengths to make sure their images remain as positive as possible.

Businesses are less than ever in control of public opinion with the advent of dozens of "review sites.". Ever since Amazon started the phenomenon of letting average consumers be the judge of what is good and not-so-good, the business world has been changed forever.

Today, every single business is totally exposed to the opinions of everyone. Businesses are naked online. Of course, this can lead to abuse, but it is not as frequent as you might think. Review sites are pretty sophisticated these days. A competitor may get away with a single scurrilous fake review, but not many of them. And, while fake negative reviews can be removed if the case can be proven, often that is very difficult. The bigger problem for businesses today is "the TRUTH." Give poor service and you will get exposed. A great many businesses don't even know they have been slammed. They are not paying attention. Those days are quickly coming to a close. Soon every business owner will be acutely aware of his or her online reputation. And, it will make their businesses better as a result.

Today, the Internet is the great equalizer. It will make good businesses better and bad businesses gone. Have you heard it said "a happy customer will tell a friend, but an unhappy customer will tell everyone he/she knows?" Well, today it is even worse. Today, many people, expecting a good experience from the business may tell a friend or two, but only a very few will take the time to write a positive review on an online site. Delivering on what you say is what they expect from your business. But, mishandle a customer, and things change dramatically. They are quick to share their negative experiences. In fact, consumers are 41 percent more likely to post a negative review online than a positive one.

So, what is a business owner to do with this new world of reputation exposure?

First, of course, is do your job. Make customer satisfaction the top priority for you and each of your employees at every level. Something else that is surprisingly easy, but not often done is, ASK! Ask how customers are experiencing your service. Of course, you will fix anything that the customer finds lacking. But, when you have a satisfied customer, ASK again. Ask a customer to take the time to provide an online review. Not everyone will, of course, but the more you ask, the greater likelihood that more will.

Your business should have a page on your web site where your customer/clients can easily access to post reviews, good and bad. Respond to every negative review, and do it online. Show anyone who is reading the reviews that you are responsive, and you are trying to resolve the issue. Reviews, good or bad, do not go away. They are there for the world to see, and your being responsive may help soften the effect of a bad review.

You should make it easy for your customer/client to post their 5-Star review to the review sites so that anytime your business shows up in an online search, your 5-Star reputation will be right there for the world to see.

A 5-Star online reputation is an asset for your business. You should be diligently working on getting a 5-Star online reputation and using it in all your marketing efforts. Do you really know what people are saying about your business or services online? If not, you can bet that potential customers/clients are seeing it. A bad reputation could lead to your business being taken out of consideration for purchases.

See Chapter 15 for Pete Goswick's biography.

CHAPTER SEVENTEEN

Use the internet to market your business and reach more people.
Steve Hamm

Traditional marketing methods are becoming both ineffective and costly. By neglecting to market your business on the web, you're missing out on the powerful business results it can provide.

In today's competitive marketplace, the need for effective online marketing solutions is more important than ever before. It is not enough to simply have a website online. In order for your business to flourish in this expansive digital marketplace, you need to incorporate a variety of online marketing strategies into the promotion and advertising activities for your business.

Effective website marketing requires some specialized skills and a working knowledge of the subtle nuances of the online world.

In this chapter we will cover the basics of online marketing, the strategies, and the different marketing methods available today. Once you understand the options available, you'll be equipped to make sound decisions related to digital marketing.

Digital Marketing: Why Every Small Business Needs it

With new websites, cellphone applications and video viewing services popping up seemingly on a daily basis, business owners must take advantage of every possible avenue to reach potential customers in order to compete for new business. Digital marketing should be an integral part of your marketing campaigns as it allows you to reach unprecedented numbers of people, with an equally unprecedented amount of accuracy.

An effective marketing strategy and campaign includes blogging, email marketing and social media. Your content for these three key areas must speak directly to the audience you want to reach. Think of digital marketing as replacing television advertising, radio and print advertising today.

Why Content Development Improves Your Marketing

Many buyers (both businesses and direct consumers) prefer to do online research before making purchases. This research often starts with search engines and then progresses to blogs and social media. Learning more about a business as well as its products and services is only natural because no one wants to make decisions without the right information.

Most buyers have come to expect businesses to employ content development in their marketing strategy. When potential customers visit your website, one of the first things they will do is look for blog posts, white papers, or a newsletter. They do this to get an idea of your level of expertise and to find out what you are like as a business. They may also want more information as to whether your product or service will meet their particular requirements. Other reasons why content is essential to your marketing efforts are outlined below:

1. Content Establishes Trust

People are more likely to buy from those they trust. Trust develops as a result of repeated exposure. This is why regular content that is published on a consistent basis is essential. Regular publishing of content turns customers into repeat buyers. It also results in a very extensive collection of information which will make the first time visitor more inclined to become a customer. Many potential customers look for evidence of expertise, and the sheer quantity and quality of your content will do this.

2. Content Starts Conversations

Having a means for the reader to react to your content in the form of a comment section on your blog, a chat box, or a contact form gets the conversation started between you and a possible customer. The type of reactions your content stimulates can be varied. Someone may express doubts or reservations or perhaps ask for more information about what you have to offer. The important thing is that your content motivated someone to go out of their way to contact you. This person is a better prospect than someone you initially contacted.

3. Content Influences Buying Decisions

This is done by publishing information that solves problems that are common to your industry. "How to" information influences the reader's thinking process as to how they can solve their particular problem. Your information can steer your prospect's thinking in directions where your services or products become the solution they are looking for.

Options for Digital Marketing

Marketing in the digital realm is constantly changing as new social media websites get added and search engines change their algorithms. The internet is a growing and expanding realm, so it makes sense to take advantage of it to reach more potential customers and spread the word about your business.

However, given that the internet is itself always changing, it's also a good idea to change along with it. In order to do this, you might have to get creative when it comes to digital marketing. Consider the following options:

1. **Email Marketing.** Email marketing has now been around for a long time, but it has also had to adapt and become more sophisticated as time goes on. In the beginning, emails couldn't even contain many graphics, but now we take these for granted. For a marketing email to stand out, it has to be more creative. It has to be well-written, personalized, succinct and visually appealing. If you've used email marketing with mixed results in the past, consider shaking things up a little bit. Go in for brighter colors and more eye-catching images. Make sure that your content is snappy and the main parts are highlighted in bold. And don't forget to make the main point of your email clear in the subject line itself.

2. **Social Media Marketing.** With the advent of social media, people can stay in touch with friends without ever leaving the security of their home. On the one hand, this is great at the level of convenience, but it can also result in a sense of isolation as people stop actually talking to each other. So while it's a good idea to expand your marketing efforts using social media, you should also continue your traditional marketing efforts which will help you stay in touch with your customers. For social media marketing to be successful, it needs to work in an interactive manner, inviting comments from customers.

3. **Blogging.** Who would have thought that the humble blog, a term that was shortened from "web log" would gain the kind of popularity it has today? The fact is that everyone likes to share what they think; blogging allows this to happen. You

too can share what's happening with your company and in your field by writing blogs or hiring a blog-writing service.

When it comes to blogging, the trick is to write about a vast variety of topics which are closely or not-so-closely related to your business. This way, you'll cast your net over a greater number of keywords and show up in a number of searches. With blogging, each person has a unique voice and writing style which is important for differentiating between all the other bloggers. For your blog to grow, you need to share 'you' and write in your own unique style; however, there is much more to it than that. Here are 4 powerful tips to take your blogging to the next level.

Stay Current with Google Updates

If you have been a blog owner for a while, chances are the terms 'Panda' and 'Penguin' are nothing new to you. The Google algorithm is constantly changing, and there is always a learning curve when it comes to improving your rankings. Unfortunately, too many people watched their websites drop from top rankings overnight because they missed out on major changes made by Google. However, with just a few tweaks, climbing back up the rankings is easy.

Guest Blogging

You are able to expand your reach by spreading your knowledge across untapped target market areas via guest blogging. Although you have likely gathered an audience for your own blog, social media circles or website, being a guest blogger provides you with opportunities to reach new audiences. Performing a little market research and browsing different blogs, you can easily find the leading authority figures in your niche or industry. These people usually have blogs that rank pretty high in Google because they are credible, honest and trustworthy. If you can catch the attention of these leaders and get their permission to post on their blogs, you can bet you will benefit from a lot of exposure.

Make your Posts Easy to Share

Enable social bookmarking icons on your blog so your content is easy to share. This allows your readers to share your posts with others. Adding action tags such as 'share this' or 'add this' makes for easy sharing. This social attention will help with SEO (search engine optimization) as well.

Understanding the dynamics of digital marketing include a few more components that are important to consider: mobile websites, responsive web design, and video marketing. Now let's take a look at these components.

Why Mobile Compatible Websites Are Growing in Business

Don't focus solely on desktop users for your business website. This will shut your business off from a major source of traffic, mobile devices. The mobile user base is constantly growing. Recently published stats show that about half of all U.S. adults now own smartphones; that figure rises to 76% for millennials. Nearly half of consumers say they won't return to a website if it doesn't load properly on their mobile devices

Since the mobile user base is large, growing and does not seem to have an end in the future, it makes sense to embrace this new direction to stay relevant to your target customers. Mobile compatible websites are dominating search engines, not only because they accommodate everyone, but because freshly-designed websites generally possess superior coding for better rankings.

Adaptive Web Design Meshes Desktop and Mobile

In order to reach mobile users, you do not need to create an entirely different website. Instead, you can utilize adaptive web design to get the proper scaling on both desktop and mobile. While this may sound complicated to those that are not familiar with web design, professional web designers can provide you with the results you need to accommodate mobile users.

Why You Should Utilize This Opportunity

Making this change is not an option anymore. Businesses cannot expect to survive for a long time if they are not willing to make adjustments that match the demands of potential and existing customers.

The Purpose of Responsive Web Design

Customers with mobile devices surfing the internet, checking emails and chatting on social media are the new wave of technology. While many people have laptops, there's nothing like having the internet in the palm of your hand. Many companies understand this. As a result, Responsive Web Design (RWD) was born for Mobile marketing.

With mobile devices changing every few years, it's hard for companies to keep track of the latest innovations. Responsive web design will do this for you. It adjusts your website to fit the size of the screen of the user's device. From 3 inches to 17.5 inches, there's no screen responsive web design cannot handle.

How does it work? It takes your website and rearranges the page so the website looks professional and practical on any screen. Responsive web design adjusts the page using other factors such as landscape/portrait orientation, screen resolution and color capacity.

Companies can create a website one time, and responsive web design will handle the rest.

Responsive web design is loved by search engines because it's easy to dissect and place on mobile and web search engines. When users click on a website that is responsive, the load time is very fast. There are no re-directions to another website or a mobile version to get the same experience; responsive web design cuts out the intermediary and takes users directly to their destination.

Responsive web design is something all companies with a website, blog or email marketing strategy need to have at their disposal. It's not one size fits all; it's one size for every device.

Gain a New Audience and More with Video Marketing

Gaining success in the online world requires a combination of many things. Some businesses strive on top-notch customer service; others provide the most competitive prices on the market. There is room for many methods to be successful. Video marketing is a method that you should consider for your business for a number of reasons. Link to video chapter

Videos Are Easy to Share

It is so simple and easy to share a video. Social media platforms have built-in ways to share videos. Sometimes all it takes is a click or two to share a video with hundreds or thousands of people. While your videos may not end up going viral, having them shared among people interested in your business should be more than enough to gain an increase in potential customers.

Videos Are Great for Gaining a Following

If you are good at making videos and people are interested in what you have to say, more likely than not, people will return for more. It is crucial to use this to your advantage, whether you start a video series that tackles specific problems, provides how-to information or delivers helpful and interesting content.

Videos Come with Extensive Analytics

There are many statistics that can be acquired from video content, which will not only help you with marketing and creating future videos, but with creating the right web content for your website. Videos are also much easier to comment on than an article, so you are more likely to get feedback on your service, website, product, or video, which can help your business improve in the future.

Conclusion

The Internet Has Changed The Way Business Is Done

Traditional outbound marketing techniques including direct mail, print advertising and telemarketing are becoming less effective. Buyers are not only finding ways to tune these messages out, but more importantly, they now have the capability to evaluate the products and services they need on their own.

As a result, businesses are transforming their marketing efforts to focus more on inbound programs that allow customers to find them. *The State of Inbound Marketing* report shows that businesses that more aggressively practice this are capturing leads more effectively. Given the digital nature of inbound marketing, the marginal cost per customer acquisition is typically close to zero. This means that as buyers continue to shift how they make purchases, the cost per lead for a given business will continue to decrease.

While it is clear that businesses are gravitating towards inbound marketing, some are moving more aggressively than others. Those who move first are more likely to reap the tremendous business benefits of this new era of marketing

The challenge for most small business owners is not only the learning curve for the new content marketing strategies but the time investment required to support effective strategies on an ongoing basis.

Seeking the help of seasoned professionals in this area may be a much more productive and wise choice.

Today, you must drive more quality traffic to your site, capture visitors as leads, nurture those leads into relationships, convert those leads into customers, and analyze the activity on your site in order to optimize all that you're doing online.

Wondering where to start? Here are 3 easy next steps.

Look at your website traffic via Google analytics. What pages are visitors landing on, for what devices, and how long do they stay on your site?

Review your current marketing strategies. What do the numbers tell you about what is working and not working? What needs to change to attract the right prospects and leads?

Assess what your competitors are doing. What other activities might you want to consider?

Steve Hamm

A marketing and business development executive with a wide range of pharmaceutical and biotechnology industry experience, Steve has been a standout contributor from his early days in marketing and sales with GlaxoSmithKline to his more recent endeavor as Owner of MaaS Pros Raleigh Durham. He has compiled a consistent record of personal achievement in developing growth strategies, revitalizing mature product lines, launching new products and generating increased sales and profits for his employers and clients.

Skilled at overcoming complex business challenges, Steve is an experienced leader with proven business instincts, vision and personal drive. He recognizes issues vital to organizational success and then focuses his team on overcoming obstacles to progress. A key personal strength is his ability to recognize, communicate and remain focused on the central issues at hand. His leadership and management skills are further complemented by an ability to leverage creative thinking into a successful business strategy.

Steve is currently the owner of MaaS Pros. MaaS Pros is a complete business solutions provider. MaaS Pros assists small to medium sized businesses in implementing profitable and measurable digital marketing solutions. His digital marketing and custom business solutions help companies "get found" online, convert visitors into qualified leads and convert those leads into sales. His main focus is to find solutions to business challenges. In order to meet these challenges, MaaS Pros utilizes their expertise in digital marketing to equip businesses with the tools they need to market themselves online using a variety of strategies.

For more information and to connect with Steve Hamm on LinkedIn visit www.linkedin.com/in/stevehamm1/. Steve also manages the Raleigh-Durham Small Business Owners and Professionals group on LinkedIn. His group is focused on small to medium sized business owners and professionals. The group's goal is to share content that is valuable and relevant to small and medium business owners, and actively network with other group members. Learn more about Maas Pros at www.maasprosraleighdurham.com.

CONCLUSION

Every day we are bombarded by so many business and marketing ideas, tactics, programs, and products that it is easy to become overwhelmed, confused, and stressed.

What if there was another way? What if the number one way to double your income in your business was right in front of you.. You just can't see it?

Why does the answer seem invisible or elusive? Because we are too busy working in the business rather than on the business. There is no time to sort through all the great ideas and strategies presented both offline and online to figure out the fastest path to grow your business and increase revenues.

We firmly believe that "Most people don't need to be taught, they just need to be reminded!" – Unknown. May this book remind you of some great ideas you perhaps have forgotten and spur you to commit to take small continuous steps to double your business.

To get more actionable tips for growing your business, visit www.17LegalWaysToDoubleYourIncome.com

Special Bonus from Diana, Earl, and Marie

Now that you've read *17 Legal Ways to Double Your Income*, you are on your way to growing your business fast! Just pick one of the ways that resonates with you and take action to implement. Don't allow yourself to become overwhelmed by all 17! Just pick one and get moving.

You'll also receive the special bonus we created to provide another big dose of business inspiration ... Diana's *30-minute interview with Larry Winget*, filled with wisdom and insights about marketing your business and Larry's 3 Rules of Business. You'll receive access to not only the audio but the written transcript.

Not sure who Larry Winget is? He is a six-time *New York Times/Wall Street Journal* bestselling author and a member of the International Speaker Hall Of Fame. He has starred in his own television series and appeared in national television commercials. Larry is also a regular contributor on many news shows on the topics of money, personal success, parenting and business. Larry is also the trademarked **Pitbull of Personal Development®.**

While this interview is offered for sale, as a special bonus you can claim it for free here:

http://17LegalWaysToDoubleYourIncome.com/bookbonus/

We are in your corner. Let us know how we can help you further. Here's to doubling your income...fast!

Best,

Diana, Earl, and Marie

Made in the USA
Columbia, SC
19 July 2017